آلْاَدْعِيَةُ الْمُنْتَخَبَةُ

مِنَ

الْحِزْبِ الْاَعْظَمُ

# Al-Hizbul A'zam

Selected Duas from Al-Hizbul A'zam

*New edition now with Salaat and Salaam and Manzil*

**From the compilation of**

Shaikh Ali ibn Sultaan Muhammad Al-Qaari *(rahmatullahi alayh)*

**Author:** Shaikh Ali ibn Sultaan Muhammad Al-Qaari *(rahmatullahi alayh)*

**Published by:**

Islamic Book Store

302 Saad Residancy

Sahin Park, M G Road

Gujarat, India

394601

Tel: 9979353876

# Contents

# INTRODUCTION

نَحْمَدُهُ وَنُصَلِّيْ عَلَى رَسُوْلِهِ الْكَرِيْم

During the mubaarak lifetime of Rasulullah ﷺ, there were many duas that he had made, imploring the help and assistance of Allah Ta'ala. These beautiful duas were preserved by the Sahaabah رضى الله عنهم and passed on to the rest of the Ummah. Many of these duas are contained in the famous compilation "Al-Hizbul A'zam" prepared by the great Muhaddith, Mullah Ali Qaari رحمه الله. For centuries people have been reading and benefitting from this great book.

In South Africa, many people from the general public expressed their desire to read and benefit from the beautiful duas of Rasulullah ﷺ. They found it a bit difficult to read the original book as it is quite lengthy and requested that selected duas be compiled and presented to the public for easy reading. Thus, it is with the *fadhal* and the Grace of Allah Ta'ala and the duas of our elders, especially our beloved ustaadh, Hadhrat Mufti Ebraheem Salehjee Saahib (daamat barakaatuhu) that the Jamiatul Ulama (KZN) Ta'limi Board has made an attempt to produce a few selected duas from the Hizbul A'zam with an easy understandable English translation.

The following are some of the specialities of this book:

1. Each day commences with the praises of Allah Ta'ala, Durood upon Rasulullah ﷺ and begging Allah Ta'ala through His beautiful names.

2. A heading for each dua has been added so that the reader may easily know what dua he is reading.

3. Duas of a similar nature have been put together, e.g. the duas of forgiveness, duas for easy rizq, duas for aafiyah, etc.

4. The Saturday section contains mainly the duas of the Ambiyaa عَلَيْهِمُ السَّلَامُ mentioned in the Qur-aan-e-Kareem.

5. The 40 Durood and Salaam has been added at the end of the booklet as the Friday section.

6. Each day's section has been divided equally, approximately 8-10 pages per day.

7. The benefits of the duas mentioned in the Hadith have also been added in the footnotes.

We make dua that Allah Ta'ala accepts this little booklet and makes it a means of gaining His closeness through these wonderful duas. Aameen.

The readers are humbly requested to please inform the publishers of any errors found in this book. Insha Allah, these errors will be rectified in the new edition.

# *SATURDAY*

## PRAISES OF ALLAH TA'ALA

اَلْحَمْدُ لِلّٰهِ رَبِّ الْعَالَمِيْنَ ، اَلرَّحْمٰنِ الرَّحِيْمِ ، مٰلِكِ يَوْمِ الدِّيْنِ ، اِيَّاكَ نَعْبُدُ وَاِيَّاكَ نَسْتَعِيْنُ ، اِهْدِنَا الصِّرَاطَ الْمُسْتَقِيْمَ ، صِرَاطَ الَّذِيْنَ اَنْعَمْتَ عَلَيْهِمْ ، غَيْرِ الْمَغْضُوْبِ عَلَيْهِمْ وَلَا الضَّآلِّيْنَ ، اٰمِيْن .

*All praise is due to Allah Ta'ala, The Master of the worlds, Most Kind, Most Merciful, Master of the Day of Judgment. You alone we worship and You alone we ask for help. Guide us to the straight path, the path of those whom You have favoured. Not of those with whom You became angered with nor (of those) who went astray. Aameen.*

## DUROOD-E-IBRAAHEEM

اَللّٰهُمَّ صَلِّ عَلٰى مُحَمَّدٍ وَّعَلٰى اٰلِ مُحَمَّدٍ كَمَا صَلَّيْتَ عَلٰى اِبْرَاهِيْمَ وَعَلٰى اٰلِ اِبْرَاهِيْمَ اِنَّكَ حَمِيْدٌ مَّجِيْدٌ . اَللّٰهُمَّ بَارِكْ عَلٰى مُحَمَّدٍ وَّعَلٰى اٰلِ مُحَمَّدٍ كَمَا بَارَكْتَ عَلٰى اِبْرَاهِيْمَ وَعَلٰى اٰلِ اِبْرَاهِيْمَ اِنَّكَ حَمِيْدٌ مَّجِيْدٌ .

*O Allah, shower Your special mercy on our Noble Master, Nabi Muhammad ﷺ and on the family of our Noble Master, Nabi*

Muhammad ﷺ just as You showered your mercy on Hadhrat Ibraahim عَلَيْهِ السَّلَام and his family. Certainly You are the Praiseworthy and the Glorious. O Allah, pour Your blessings on our Noble Master, Nabi Muhammad ﷺ and on the family of our Noble Master, Nabi Muhammad ﷺ just as You blessed Hadhrat Ibraahim عَلَيْهِ السَّلَام and his family. Certainly You are Praiseworthy and Glorious.

## BEGGING FROM ALLAH TA'ALA THROUGH HIS BEAUTIFUL NAMES

يَا مُؤْنِسَ كُلِّ وَحِيْدٍ، وَيَا صَاحِبَ كُلِّ فَرِيْدٍ، وَيَا قَرِيْبًا غَيْرَ بَعِيْدٍ، وَيَا شَاهِدًا غَيْرَ غَائِبٍ، وَيَا غَالِبًا غَيْرَ مَغْلُوْبٍ، يَا حَيُّ يَا قَيُّوْمُ، يَا ذَا الْجَلَالِ وَالْاِكْرَامِ

O The Comforter and Companion of every lonely person, O The One who is near and never far, O The One who is present and never absent, O You who overpowers all but is never overpowered in any way, O The Everlasting and Sustainer, The Majestic and Most Honoured.

## DUA FOR GOODNESS IN THIS WORLD AND THE NEXT

رَبَّنَا اٰتِنَا فِي الدُّنْيَا حَسَنَةً وَّفِي الْاٰخِرَةِ حَسَنَةً وَّقِنَا عَذَابَ النَّارِ

O Allah, grant us the good of this world and the good of the Hereafter and save us from the punishment of the fire.

# DUA FOR ACCEPTANCE[1]

رَبَّنَا تَقَبَّلْ مِنَّا، إِنَّكَ أَنْتَ السَّمِيعُ الْعَلِيمُ، وَتُبْ عَلَيْنَا، إِنَّكَ أَنْتَ التَّوَّابُ الرَّحِيمُ

*O Allah, accept from us (our good actions), certainly You are all Hearing and all Knowing. Accept our taubah (repentance). Certainly You are Most Forgiving and Most Merciful.*

## DUA FOR PATIENCE AND STEADFASTNESS

رَبَّنَا أَفْرِغْ عَلَيْنَا صَبْرًا وَّثَبِّتْ أَقْدَامَنَا وَانْصُرْنَا عَلَى الْقَوْمِ الْكَٰفِرِينَ

*O Allah, pour sabr (patience) in us, keep our feet firm and help us against the unbelievers.*

## DUA FOR DEATH ON IMAAN

رَبَّنَا لَا تُزِغْ قُلُوبَنَا بَعْدَ إِذْ هَدَيْتَنَا وَهَبْ لَنَا مِنْ لَّدُنْكَ رَحْمَةً إِنَّكَ أَنْتَ الْوَهَّابُ

*O Allah! Do not let our hearts go astray after You have guided us, and grant us mercy from Your side. Certainly You are The Great Giver of favours.*

---

[1] This dua was made by Hadhrat Ibraheem عَلَيْهِ السَّلَام when he built the Ka'bah Shareef

## DUA FOR PIOUS CHILDREN

رَبِّ هَبْ لِيْ مِنْ لَّدُنْكَ ذُرِّيَّةً طَيِّبَةً اِنَّكَ سَمِيْعُ الدُّعَاءِ

*O Allah, bless me from Your side with good children. Certainly You hear all duas.*

## DUA FOR FORGIVENESS AND STEADFASTNESS

رَبَّنَا اغْفِرْ لَنَا ذُنُوْبَنَا وَاِسْرَافَنَا فِيْ اَمْرِنَا وَثَبِّتْ اَقْدَامَنَا وَانْصُرْنَا عَلَى الْقَوْمِ الْكِفِرِيْنَ

*O Allah, forgive our sins and forgive us for overstepping the mark, keep our feet firm and help us against the disbelievers.*

## DUA FOR FORGIVENESS AND PROTECTION FROM DISGRACE ON THE DAY OF QIYAAMAH

رَبَّنَا فَاغْفِرْ لَنَا ذُنُوْبَنَا وَكَفِّرْ عَنَّا سَيِّئَاتِنَا وَتَوَفَّنَا مَعَ الْاَبْرَارِ، رَبَّنَا وَاٰتِنَا مَا وَعَدْتَّنَا عَلَى رُسُلِكَ وَلَا تُخْزِنَا يَوْمَ الْقِيَامَةِ . اِنَّكَ لَا تُخْلِفُ الْمِيْعَادَ

*O Allah, forgive our sins and pardon our wrongs and when removing our souls, include us among the righteous. O Allah, grant us what You have promised us through Your Messengers and do not disgrace us on the Day of Qiyaamah. Verily You do not break Your promise.*

## Dua for Forgiveness[1]

رَبَّنَا ظَلَمْنَآ اَنْفُسَنَا وَاِنْ لَّمْ تَغْفِرْ لَنَا وَتَرْحَمْنَا لَنَكُوْنَنَّ مِنَ الْخَاسِرِيْنَ

*O Allah, we have wronged ourselves and if You do not forgive us and have mercy on us, we shall certainly be from the losers.*

## Dua for Forgiveness and Protection

رَبِّ اغْفِرْ لِيْ وَلِاَخِيْ وَاَدْخِلْنَا فِيْ رَحْمَتِكَ وَاَنْتَ اَرْحَمُ الرَّاحِمِيْنَ ۔ عَلَى اللهِ

تَوَكَّلْنَا رَبَّنَا لَا تَجْعَلْنَا فِتْنَةً لِّلْقَوْمِ الظَّالِمِيْنَ وَنَجِّنَا بِرَحْمَتِكَ مِنَ الْقَوْمِ

الْكٰفِرِيْنَ

*O Allah, forgive me and my brother and enter us into Your mercy. You are The Most Merciful. We place our trust in Allah. O Allah, do not make us a victim for the cruel ones and save us, through Your mercy, from the disbelievers.*

## Dua for death on Imaan and staying in the company of the pious[2]

فَاطِرَ السَّمٰوٰتِ وَالْاَرْضِ اَنْتَ وَلِيّْ فِي الدُّنْيَا وَالْاٰخِرَةِ تَوَفَّنِيْ مُسْلِمًا

---

[1] This dua was made by Hadhrat Aadam عَلَيْهِ السَّلَام when he was removed from Jannah.

[2] This dua was made by Hadhrat Yusuf عَلَيْهِ السَّلَام towards the end of his life

وَّاَلْحِقْنِيْ بِالصَّالِحِيْنَ ، اِنَّ رَبِّيْ لَسَمِيْعُ الدُّعَآءِ

*O The Maker of the skies and the earth, You are my guardian in this world and the hereafter. Cause me to die as a Muslim and join me with the pious. Certainly, my Rabb hears all duas.*

## DUA FOR ESTABLISHING SALAAH AND FORGIVENESS FOR OURSELVES, OUR PARENTS AND FOR ALL MUSLIMS

رَبِّ اجْعَلْنِيْ مُقِيْمَ الصَّلٰوةِ وَمِنْ ذُرِّيَّتِيْ رَبَّنَا وَتَقَبَّلْ دُعَآءِ . رَبَّنَا اغْفِرْ لِيْ وَلِوَالِدَيَّ وَلِلْمُؤْمِنِيْنَ يَوْمَ يَقُوْمُ الْحِسَابُ

*O Allah, make me and my children from those who establish salaah and accept my duas. O Allah, forgive me, my parents and all the Muslims on the Day of Reckoning.*

## DUA FOR ALLAH'S MERCY AND EASE TO FULFIL ONES AIMS

رَبَّنَا اٰتِنَا مِنْ لَّدُنْكَ رَحْمَةً وَّهَيِّئْ لَنَا مِنْ اَمْرِنَا رَشَدًا

*O Allah, grant us Your mercy and make it easy for us to fulfill our aims.*

# DUA FOR EASE IN ONE'S MATTERS[1]

رَبِّ اشْرَحْ لِيْ صَدْرِيْ وَيَسِّرْ لِيْ اَمْرِيْ

*O Allah, open up my heart and make my work easy for me.*

# DUA FOR INCREASE IN ILM

رَبِّ زِدْنِيْ عِلْمًا

*O Allah, increase me in knowledge.*

# DUA FOR FORGIVENESS[2]

لَا اِلٰهَ اِلَّا اَنْتَ سُبْحَانَكَ اِنِّيْ كُنْتُ مِنَ الظَّالِمِيْنَ

*There is no god besides You, You are Pure from all faults, definitely I am from the sinners.*

# DUA FOR A WIFE AND FOR CHILDREN WHO WILL BE A COOLNESS TO YOUR EYES

رَبَّنَا هَبْ لَنَا مِنْ اَزْوَاجِنَا وَذُرِّيَّاتِنَا قُرَّةَ اَعْيُنٍ وَّاجْعَلْنَا لِلْمُتَّقِيْنَ اِمَامًا

---

[1] Dua made by Hadhrat Moosa عَلَيْهِ السَّلَام before he went to Firaun to invite him to Islam.

[2] Dua was made by Hadhrat Yunus عَلَيْهِ السَّلَام when he was trapped in the stomach of the fish.

*O Allah, grant us such wives and children who will be a source of coolness (delight) to our eyes and make us the leaders of pious people.*

## DUA FOR CHILDREN

رَبِّ لَا تَذَرْنِيْ فَرْدًا وَّاَنْتَ خَيْرُ الْوَارِثِيْنَ

*O Allah, do not leave me alone; You are the Best of protectors.*

## DUA FOR PIOUS CHILDREN

رَبِّ هَبْ لِيْ مِنَ الصَّالِحِيْنَ

*O Allah, grant me pious children.*

## DUA FOR GOODNESS[1]

رَبِّ اِنِّيْ لِمَا اَنْزَلْتَ اِلَيَّ مِنْ خَيْرٍ فَقِيْرٌ

*O Allah, I am desperately in need of whatever good You have in store for me.*

## DUA FOR WISDOM, GOOD COMPANY, PIOUS CHILDREN AND JANNAH[2]

رَبِّ هَبْ لِيْ حُكْمًا وَّاَلْحِقْنِيْ بِالصَّالِحِيْنَ ۰ وَاجْعَلْ لِّيْ لِسَانَ صِدْقٍ فِي

---

[1] This dua was made by Hadhrat Moosa عَلَيْهِ السَّلَام

[2] This dua was made by Hadhrat Ibraaheem عَلَيْهِ السَّلَام

الْاٰخِرِيْنَ وَاجْعَلْنِيْ مِنْ وَّرَثَةِ جَنَّةِ النَّعِيْمِ

*O Allah, bless me with wisdom and join me with the pious. Grant me a reputation of truthfulness in generations to come. Make me among those who will inherit the garden of bliss (Jannah).*

## DUA FOR PROTECTION FROM JAHANNAM

رَبَّنَا اصْرِفْ عَنَّا عَذَابَ جَهَنَّمَ اِنَّ عَذَابَهَا كَانَ غَرَامًا. اِنَّهَا سَاءَتْ مُسْتَقَرًّا وَّمُقَامًا

*O Allah, turn away the punishment of Jahannam from us. Certainly its punishment is indeed dreadful. Undoubtedly it is an evil place for staying and resting.*

## DUA OF SHUKR (APPRECIATION)[1]

رَبِّ اَوْزِعْنِيْ اَنْ اَشْكُرَ نِعْمَتَكَ الَّتِيْ اَنْعَمْتَ عَلَيَّ وَعَلٰى وَالِدَيَّ وَاَنْ اَعْمَلَ صَالِحًا تَرْضٰهُ وَاَدْخِلْنِيْ بِرَحْمَتِكَ فِيْ عِبَادِكَ الصَّالِحِيْنَ

*O Allah, make me grateful to You for Your favours that You have bestowed me and my parents, and (grant me the ability) to do such actions that will please You. O Allah (Please) include me, through Your mercy, amongst Your pious servants.*

---

[1] This dua was made by Hadhrat Sulaymaan عَلَيْهِ السَّلَام

## DUA FOR FORGIVENESS

رَبِّ اِنِّيْ ظَلَمْتُ نَفْسِيْ فَاغْفِرْ لِيْ

*O Allah, I have oppressed myself, please forgive me.*

## DUA FOR FORGIVENESS OF THOSE WHO HAVE PASSED AWAY AND DUA FOR A CLEAN HEART

رَبَّنَا اغْفِرْ لَنَا وَلِاِخْوَانِنَا الَّذِيْنَ سَبَقُوْنَا بِالْاِيْمَانِ وَلَا تَجْعَلْ فِيْ قُلُوْبِنَا غِلًّا لِّلَّذِيْنَ اٰمَنُوْا رَبَّنَا اِنَّكَ رَءُوْفٌ رَّحِيْمٌ

*O Allah, forgive us and our Muslim brothers who have passed away with Imaan and do not allow us to have any ill feelings in our hearts towards any Muslims. O Allah, You are Most Kind and Merciful.*

## DUA FOR FORGIVENESS OF ONE'S PARENTS AND FOR ANYONE WHO ENTERS ONE'S HOME[1]

رَبِّ اغْفِرْ لِيْ وَلِوَالِدَيَّ وَلِمَنْ دَخَلَ بَيْتِيَ مُؤْمِنًا وَّلِلْمُؤْمِنِيْنَ وَالْمُؤْمِنَاتِ

*O Allah, forgive me, my parents, and those Muslims who have entered my house as well as all the Muslim men and women.*

---

[1] This dua was made by Hadhrat Nooh عَلَيْهِ السَّلَام

## SUNDAY

### PRAISES OF ALLAH TA'ALA

اَللّٰهُمَّ لَكَ الْحَمْدُ كُلُّهُ، وَلَكَ الشُّكْرُ كُلُّهُ، وَلَكَ الْمُلْكُ كُلُّهُ، وَلَكَ الْخَلْقُ كُلُّهُ، بِيَدِكَ الْخَيْرُ كُلُّهُ، وَاِلَيْكَ يَرْجِعُ الْاَمْرُ كُلُّهُ

*O Allah, all praise and gratitude is for You, the entire kingdom and creation belong to You. All good is in Your hands and all matters ultimately return to You.*

### DUROOD UPON RASULULLAH ﷺ

اَللّٰهُمَّ صَلِّ عَلٰى رُوْحِ مُحَمَّدٍ فِي الْاَرْوَاحِ، وَصَلِّ عَلٰى جَسَدِ مُحَمَّدٍ فِي الْاَجْسَادِ، وَصَلِّ عَلٰى قَبْرِ مُحَمَّدٍ فِي الْقُبُوْرِ

*O Allah, send Your special mercy on the soul of our Noble Master Nabi Muhammad ﷺ among all human souls, send Your special mercy on the body of our Noble Master Muhammad ﷺ, among all bodies, send Your special mercy on the grave of our Noble Master Muhammad ﷺ, among all the graves.*

### BEGGING ALLAH TA'ALA THROUGH HIS BEAUTIFUL NAMES

يَا نُوْرَ السَّمٰوَاتِ وَالْاَرْضِ، يَا زَيْنَ السَّمٰوَاتِ وَالْاَرْضِ، يَا جَبَّارَ السَّمٰوَاتِ

وَالْاَرْضِ، يَا عِمَادَ السَّمٰوَاتِ وَالْاَرْضِ، يَا بَدِيْعَ السَّمٰوَاتِ وَالْاَرْضِ، يَا قَيَّامَ السَّمٰوَاتِ وَالْاَرْضِ، يَاذَا الْجَلَالِ وَالْاِكْرَامِ

O The One who is the light of the heavens and the earth. O The One who is the beauty of the heavens and the earth. O The Mighty King of the heavens and earth. O The Supporter of the heavens and earth. O The Originator of the heavens and earth. O The Sustainer of the heavens and earth. O The Majestic and Kind.

## DUA FOR IMAAN AND YAQEEN

اَللّٰهُمَّ اِنِّيْ اَسْاَلُكَ اِيْمَانًا يُّبَاشِرُ قَلْبِيْ، وَيَقِيْنًا صَادِقًا حَتّٰى اَعْلَمَ اَنَّهُ لَا يُصِيْبُنِيْ اِلَّا مَا كَتَبْتَ لِيْ، وَرِضًا بِمَا قَسَمْتَ لِيْ اِنَّكَ عَلٰى كُلِّ شَيْءٍ قَدِيْرٌ

O Allah, I beg of You to bless me with such Imaan that enters deeply into my heart and the proper yaqeen (firm belief) which will cause me to realise that whatever happens to me was already decided by You for me. Allow me to be pleased with whatever You have written for me. Certainly You have power over everything.

## DUA FOR STRONG IMAAN, A FEARFUL HEART, TRUE YAQEEN AND FIRMNESS IN DEEN

اَللّٰهُمَّ اِنِّيْ اَسْاَلُكَ اِيْمَانًا دَائِمًا وَاَسْاَلُكَ قَلْبًا خَاشِعًا. وَاَسْاَلُكَ يَقِيْنًا صَادِقًا. وَاَسْاَلُكَ دِيْنًا قَيِّمًا

*O Allah, I beg of You (to bless me with) Imaan which remains forever, and I ask You for a humble heart and true belief and I ask You for firmness in Deen.*

## DUA FOR STRONG IMAAN, GUIDANCE AND BENEFICIAL KNOWLEDGE

اَللّٰهُمَّ اِنِّیْ اَسْاَلُكَ اِیْمَانًا دَائِمًا وَّهُدًی قَیِّمًا وَّعِلْمًا نَّافِعًا

*O Allah, I beg of You for Imaan that remains forever, correct guidance and beneficial knowledge.*

## DUA FOR STRONG IMAAN, NEVER-ENDING FAVOURS AND THE COMPANIONSHIP OF RASULULLAH ﷺ IN JANNAH

اَللّٰهُمَّ اِنِّیْ اَسْاَلُكَ اِیْمَانًا لَّا یَرْتَدُّ ، وَنَعِیْمًا لَّا یَنْفَدُ ، وَمُرَافَقَةَ نَبِیِّنَا مُحَمَّدٍ صَلَّی اللّٰهُ عَلَیْهِ وَسَلَّمَ فِیْ اَعْلٰی دَرَجَةِ الْجَنَّةِ ، جَنَّةِ الْخُلْدِ

*O Allah, I beg of You to bless me with Imaan which does not leave, favours which never end and the company of our beloved Nabi Muhammad ﷺ in the highest stages of Jannah.*

## DUA FOR BEAUTIFUL IMAAN AND HIDAAYAT (GUIDANCE)

اَللّٰهُمَّ زَیِّنَّا بِزِیْنَةِ الْاِیْمَانِ وَاجْعَلْنَا هُدَاةً مُّهْتَدِیْنَ

*O Allah, beautify us with the beauty of Imaan, guide us and make us guides for others as well (to the right path).*

## DUA FOR IMAAN TO BECOME BELOVED TO US

اَللّٰهُمَّ حَبِّبْ اِلَيْنَا الْاِيْمَانَ وَزَيِّنْهُ فِيْ قُلُوْبِنَا وَكَرِّهْ اِلَيْنَا الْكُفْرَ وَالْفُسُوْقَ وَالْعِصْيَانَ وَاجْعَلْنَا مِنَ الرَّاشِدِيْنَ

*O Allah, make Imaan beloved to us and beautify our hearts with it and make us hate kufr (disbelief), immorality and sin and include us from the pious.*

## DUA FOR PROTECTION FROM KUFR, POVERTY AND PUNISHMENT IN THE GRAVE

اَللّٰهُمَّ اِنِّيْ اَعُوْذُبِكَ مِنَ الْكُفْرِ وَالْفَقْرِ ، اَللّٰهُمَّ اِنِّيْ اَعُوْذُبِكَ مِنْ عَذَابِ الْقَبْرِ لَا اِلٰهَ اِلَّا اَنْتَ

*O Allah, I seek Your protection from (kufr) disbelief and poverty. O Allah, I seek Your protection from being punished in the grave. There is no God besides You.*

## DUA FOR IMAAN AND GOOD AKHLAAQ

اَللّٰهُمَّ اِنِّيْ اَسْاَلُكَ صِحَّةً فِيْ اِيْمَانٍ، وَاِيْمَانًا فِيْ حُسْنِ خُلُقٍ، وَنَجَاةً يَّتْبَعُهَا

فَلَاحٌ، وَّرَحْمَةً مِّنْكَ وَعَافِيَةً وَّ مَغْفِرَةً مِّنْكَ وَرِضْوَانًا

*O Allah, I beg of You for perfect Imaan, such Imaan which has good manners, a good life (in this world) followed by complete success (in the Hereafter). I beg of Your mercy, peace and forgiveness and (I beg) for Your pleasure.*

## DUAS FOR THE FORGIVENESS AND MERCY OF ALLAH TA'ALA

اَللّٰهُمَّ اغْفِرْ لِيْ وَارْحَمْنِيْ وَاَدْخِلْنِيْ الْجَنَّةَ

*O Allah, forgive me, have mercy on me and enter me into Jannah.*

اَللّٰهُمَّ اعْفُ عَنِّيْ فَاِنَّكَ عَفُوٌّ كَرِيْمٌ

*O, Allah, forgive me as You are Most Kind and most Forgiving.*

اَللّٰهُمَّ اغْفِرْ لِيْ وَارْحَمْنِيْ وَتُبْ عَلَيَّ اِنَّكَ اَنْتَ التَّوَّابُ الرَّحِيْمُ

*O Allah, forgive me, have mercy on me, accept my taubah (repentance), certainly You are Most Forgiving and Most Merciful.*

رَبَّنَا لَا تُؤَاخِذْنَا اِنْ نَّسِيْنَا اَوْ اَخْطَأْنَا. رَبَّنَا وَلَا تَحْمِلْ عَلَيْنَا اِصْرًا كَمَا حَمَلْتَهٗ عَلَى الَّذِيْنَ مِنْ قَبْلِنَا. رَبَّنَا وَلَا تُحَمِّلْنَا مَا لَا طَاقَةَ لَنَا بِهٖ وَاعْفُ عَنَّا وَاغْفِرْ لَنَا وَارْحَمْنَا. اَنْتَ مَوْلَانَا فَانْصُرْنَا عَلَى الْقَوْمِ الْكٰفِرِيْنَ

*O Allah do not punish us for the sins we did by mistake or in error. Do not load us with such heavy duties which had been placed on the people before us. O Allah, do not load us with that which we cannot manage. Overlook our sins, Forgive us and have mercy on us. You are our Master so help us against the disbelievers.*

رَبِّ اغْفِرْ وَارْحَمْ وَاَنْتَ خَيْرُ الرَّاحِمِيْنَ

*O Allah, forgive us and have mercy upon us. Certainly You are the best of those who show Mercy.*

رَبَّنَا اٰمَنَّا فَاغْفِرْ لَنَا وَارْحَمْنَا وَاَنْتَ خَيْرُ الرَّاحِمِيْنَ

*O Allah, we have brought Imaan, forgive us and have mercy on us and You are the best of those who show Mercy.*

## SAYYIDUL ISTIGHFAAR

سَيِّدُ الْاِسْتِغْفَارِ: اَللّٰهُمَّ اَنْتَ رَبِّيْ لَا اِلٰهَ اِلَّا اَنْتَ خَلَقْتَنِيْ وَاَنَا عَبْدُكَ وَاَنَا عَلٰى عَهْدِكَ وَوَعْدِكَ مَا اسْتَطَعْتُ، اَعُوْذُ بِكَ مِنْ شَرِّ مَا صَنَعْتُ، اَبُوْءُ لَكَ بِنِعْمَتِكَ عَلَيَّ وَاَبُوْءُ بِذَنْبِيْ فَاغْفِرْ لِيْ فَاِنَّهٗ لَا يَغْفِرُ الذُّنُوْبَ اِلَّا اَنْتَ

*O Allah, You are my Rabb, there is no god besides You. You have created me and I am Your servant. As far as possible I try to fulfill the promises (which I made to You). I seek Your protection from the evil of my sins. I fully acknowledge the favours You have given to me and I admit my mistakes. Please forgive me since no one besides You can forgive sins.*

اَللّٰهُمَّ اَسْتَغْفِرُكَ لِذَنْبِيْ وَاَسْاَلُكَ رَحْمَتَكَ

*O Allah, I beg You to forgive my sins and I beg of You for Your mercy.*

اَللّٰهُمَّ اغْفِرْ لِيْ ذَنْبِيْ كُلَّهُ دِقَّهُ وَجِلَّهُ وَاَوَّلَهُ وَاٰخِرَهُ وَعَلَانِيَتَهُ وَسِرَّهُ

*O Allah, forgive all my sins, small and big, the first and the last, and those which I did openly or secretly.*

## DUA FOR FORGIVENESS[10]

اَللّٰهُمَّ اِنِّيْ ظَلَمْتُ نَفْسِيْ ظُلْمًا كَثِيْرًا وَّلَا يَغْفِرُ الذُّنُوْبَ اِلَّا اَنْتَ فَاغْفِرْ لِيْ مَغْفِرَةً مِّنْ عِنْدِكَ وَارْحَمْنِيْ اِنَّكَ اَنْتَ الْغَفُوْرُ الرَّحِيْمُ

*O Allah, I have seriously wronged myself and no one besides You can forgive sins, so forgive me and have mercy on me. Certainly You are Most Forgiving and Most Merciful.*

رَبَّنَا اِنَّنَآ اٰمَنَّا فَاغْفِرْ لَنَا ذُنُوْبَنَا وَكَفِّرْ عَنَّا سَيِّاٰتِنَا وَتَوَفَّنَا مَعَ الْاَبْرَارِ

*O Allah, we have brought Imaan, forgive our sins and overlook our mistakes and allow us to die with the righteous.*

---

[10] This dua was taught to Hadhrat Abu Bakr رضى الله عنه by Rasulullah ﷺ

## DUA FOR AN EASY QUESTIONING

اَللّٰهُمَّ حَاسِبْنِيْ حِسَابًا يَّسِيْرًا

*O Allah, put me through an easy questioning.*

## DUA FOR HELP IN MAKING ZIKR, SHUKR AND GOOD DEEDS

اَللّٰهُمَّ اَعِنِّيْ عَلٰى ذِكْرِكَ وَ شُكْرِكَ وَ حُسْنِ عِبَادَتِكَ

*O Allah, help me in remembering You, being grateful to You and worshipping You well.*

## MONDAY

### PRAISES OF ALLAH TA'ALA

اَللّٰهُمَّ لَكَ الْحَمْدُ مِلْءَ السَّمٰوَاتِ وَمِلْءَ الْاَرْضِ وَمِلْءَ مَا بَيْنَهُمَا وَمِلْءَ مَا شِئْتَ مِنْ شَيْءٍ بَعْدُ اَنْتَ اَهْلُ الثَّنَاءِ وَالْكِبْرِيَاءِ وَالْمَجْدِ اَحَقُّ مَا قَالَ الْعَبْدُ وَكُلُّنَا لَكَ عَبْدٌ لَا مَانِعَ لِمَا اَعْطَيْتَ وَلَا مُعْطِيَ لِمَا مَنَعْتَ وَلَا رَادَّ لِمَا قَضَيْتَ وَلَا يَنْفَعُ ذَا الْجَدِّ مِنْكَ الْجَدُّ

*O Allah, all praise be to You in quantities equal to the heavens and the earth, what is inbetween them and whatever is beyond them as You may wish. You alone deserve to be praised, glorified and honoured. Whatever Your slave has said is true, and we are all Your slaves. No one can stop what You give and no one can give what You hold back. No one can return what You have decided and the wealth of the wealthy in front of You (O Allah) is of no benefit to them.*

### DUROOD UPON RASULULLAH ﷺ

اَللّٰهُمَّ صَلِّ عَلٰى مُحَمَّدٍ كُلَّمَا ذَكَرَهُ الذَّاكِرُوْنَ ، وَصَلِّ عَلٰى مُحَمَّدٍ كُلَّمَا غَفَلَ عَنْ ذِكْرِهِ الْغَافِلُوْنَ

*O Allah, send Your special mercy on our Noble Master, Nabi Muhammad ﷺ whenever people remember and mention his name and send*

*Your special mercy on our Noble Master, Nabi Muhammad صَلَّى اللهُ عَلَيْهِ وَسَلَّمَ whenever careless people fail to remember and mention him.*

## BEGGING ALLAH TA'ALA THROUGH HIS BEAUTIFUL NAMES

يَا صَرِيْخَ الْمُسْتَصْرِخِيْنَ، وَمُنْتَهَى الْعَائِذِيْنَ وَالْمُفَرِّجَ عَنِ الْمَكْرُوْبِيْنَ وَالْمُرَوِّحَ عَنِ الْمَغْمُوْمِيْنَ وَمُجِيْبَ دُعَاءِ الْمُضْطَرِّيْنَ، وَيَا كَاشِفَ الْكَرَبِ يَا اِلٰهَ الْعَالَمِيْنَ، وَيَا اَرْحَمَ الرَّاحِمِيْنَ مَنْزُوْلٌ بِكَ كُلُّ حَاجَةٍ

*O The One who answers the duas of people and is the highest (place of protection) for those who seek protection, O You Who opens the way for those in discomfort, soothes the sorrow of the grieving and answers the duas of those in difficulty. O The One who removes all difficulties. O The Rabb of the worlds. O The One who is Most Merciful and Compassionate, we humbly place all our needs before You.*

## DUA FOR KNOWLEDGE, TOLERANCE, TAQWA AND AAFIYAH

اَللّٰهُمَّ اَغْنِنِيْ بِالْعِلْمِ، وَزَيِّنِّيْ بِالْحِلْمِ، وَاَكْرِمْنِيْ بِالتَّقْوٰى، وَجَمِّلْنِيْ بِالْعَافِيَةِ

*O Allah, enrich me with knowledge, beautify me with tolerance, honour me with piety and beautify me with good health.*

## Dua for Beneficial Knowledge, Sustenance, and Shifa

اَللّٰهُمَّ اِنِّيْ اَسْاَلُكَ عِلْمًا نَافِعًا وَّرِزْقًا وَّاسِعًا وَّشِفَاءً مِّنْ كُلِّ دَاءٍ

*O Allah, I beg You for beneficial knowledge, abundant sustenance and cure from all illnesses.*

## Dua for Pure Sustenance, Beneficial Knowledge and Accepted Actions

اَللّٰهُمَّ اِنِّيْ اَسْاَلُكَ رِزْقًا طَيِّبًا وَّعِلْمًا نَّافِعًا وَّعَمَلًا مُّتَقَبَّلًا

*O Allah, I beg You for Halaal (pure) sustenance, beneficial knowledge and actions that are accepted.*

## Dua for opening up the doors of Mercy and Rizq

اَللّٰهُمَّ افْتَحْ لَنَا اَبْوَابَ رَحْمَتِكَ وَسَهِّلْ لَّنَا اَبْوَابَ رِزْقِكَ

*O Allah, open the gates of Your mercy for us and make easy for us the doors of Your sustenance.*

## Dua for increasing in ones Rizq

اَللّٰهُمَّ اجْعَلْ اَوْسَعَ رِزْقِكَ عَلَيَّ عِنْدَ كِبَرِ سِنِّيْ. وَانْقِطَاعِ عُمْرِيْ

*O Allah, make my rizq (sustenance) the most abundant during my old age*

*and at the last part of my life.*

## DUA-UL KURAB (FOR A PERSON IN HARDSHIP)

اَللّٰهُمَّ رَحْمَتَكَ اَرْجُوْ ، فَلَا تَكِلْنِيْ اِلٰى نَفْسِيْ طَرْفَةَ عَيْنٍ ، وَاَصْلِحْ لِيْ شَاْنِيْ كُلَّهٗ ، لَا اِلٰهَ اِلَّا اَنْتَ

*O Allah, I am hopeful of Your mercy, so do not leave me to myself for the blink of an eye and make all my work easy. There is no god besides You.*

## DUA FOR HELP AND ASSISTANCE [1]

يَا حَيُّ يَا قَيُّوْمُ بِرَحْمَتِكَ اَسْتَغِيْثُ

*O Allah, The Everlasting, The Sustainer, I sincerely beg Your mercy.*

## DUA FOR THE LOVE OF ALLAH TA'ALA

اَللّٰهُمَّ اجْعَلْ حُبَّكَ اَحَبَّ الْاَشْيَاءِ اِلَيَّ ، وَاجْعَلْ خَشْيَتَكَ اَخْوَفَ الْاَشْيَاءِ عِنْدِيْ ، وَاقْطَعْ عَنِّيْ حَاجَاتِ الدُّنْيَا بِالشَّوْقِ اِلٰى لِقَائِكَ ، وَاِذَا اَقْرَرْتَ اَعْيُنَ اَهْلِ الدُّنْيَا مِنْ دُنْيَاهُمْ فَاَقْرِرْ عَيْنِيْ مِنْ عِبَادَتِكَ

*O Allah, make Your love the most beloved of things to me and make Your fear the most fearful of things to me. Remove all worldly needs from my*

---

[1] This dua was made by Rasulullah ﷺ for the entire night of Badar

heart by filling it with a burning desire for meeting with You. And when You cool the eyes of the worldly people with their worldly jobs then cool my eyes with acts of ibaadah (worship) towards You.

## Dua for a clean heart

اَللّٰهُمَّ اغْفِرْ لِلْمُؤْمِنِيْنَ وَالْمُؤْمِنَاتِ وَالْمُسْلِمِيْنَ وَالْمُسْلِمَاتِ، اَلْاَحْيَاءِ مِنْهُمْ وَالْاَمْوَاتِ، وَلِاِخْوَانِنَا الَّذِيْنَ سَبَقُوْنَا بِالْاِيْمَانِ، وَلَا تَجْعَلْ فِيْ قُلُوْبِنَا غِلًّا لِّلَّذِيْنَ اٰمَنُوْا رَبَّنَا اِنَّكَ رَءُوْفٌ رَّحِيْمٌ

O Allah, forgive me and all the believing men and women, all the Muslim men and women including those who are alive and those who have passed away and our Muslim brothers who lived before us, and (O Allah) do not leave any bad-feelings in our hearts towards the Muslims. Certainly You are Most Kind and all Merciful.

## Dua for Sabr, Shukar and for Respect

اَللّٰهُمَّ اجْعَلْنِيْ صَبُوْرًا، وَاجْعَلْنِيْ شَكُوْرًا، وَاجْعَلْنِيْ فِيْ عَيْنِيْ صَغِيْرًا وَفِيْ اَعْيُنِ النَّاسِ كَبِيْرًا

O Allah, make me patient and make me be grateful to You. Make me look small in my eyes but great in the eyes of others.

## Dua for Beneficial Knowledge, Accepted Actions and Pure Rizq

اَللّٰهُمَّ اِنِّيْ اَسْاَلُكَ عِلْمًا نَّافِعًا وَّعَمَلًا مُّتَقَبَّلًا وَّرِزْقًا حَلَالًا طَيِّبًا

*O Allah, I beg You to bless me with beneficial knowledge, actions that are accepted, and pure halaal sustenance.*

## Dua for Humility

اَللّٰهُمَّ اَحْيِنِيْ مِسْكِيْنًا وَّاَمِتْنِيْ مِسْكِيْنًا وَّاحْشُرْنِيْ فِيْ زُمْرَةِ الْمَسَاكِيْن

*O Allah, allow me to live as a humble person, cause me to die as a humble person and raise me (on the Day of Qiyaamah) in the company of the humble ones.*

## Dua for Taufeeq (Ability) to do good actions

اَللّٰهُمَّ اِنِّيْ اَسْاَلُكَ التَّوْفِيْقَ لِمَحَابِّكَ مِنَ الْاَعْمَالِ وَصِدْقَ التَّوَكُّلِ عَلَيْكَ وَحُسْنَ الظَّنِّ بِكَ

*O Allah, I beg You for the ability to do those actions which are pleasing to You, true reliance on You and I ask of You to bless me with good thoughts about You.*

## DUA FOR EASE AT THE TIME OF DIFFICULTY

اَللّٰهُمَّ الْطُفْ بِيْ فِيْ تَيْسِيْرِ كُلِّ عَسِيْرٍ، فَاِنَّ تَيْسِيْرَ كُلِّ عَسِيْرٍ عَلَيْكَ يَسِيْرٌ وَاَسْأَلُكَ الْيُسْرَ وَالْمُعَافَاةَ فِي الدُّنْيَا وَالْاٰخِرَةِ

*O Allah, be kind to me by making every difficulty easy for me as it is absolutely easy for You to do so. And I ask You for ease and forgiveness in this world and the aakhirah.*

## DUA FOR PROTECTION FROM SHAMELESS ACTIONS

اَللّٰهُمَّ حَصِّنْ فَرْجِيْ، وَيَسِّرْ لِيْ اَمْرِيْ

*O Allah, guard my private parts and make my work easy for me.*

## DUA FOR A PERFECT WUDHU AND A PERFECT SALAAH

اَللّٰهُمَّ اِنِّيْ اَسْأَلُكَ تَمَامَ الْوُضُوْءِ وَتَمَامَ الصَّلَاةِ وَتَمَامَ رِضْوَانِكَ، وَتَمَامَ مَغْفِرَتِكَ

*O Allah, I beg You to grant me perfection in wudhu, perfection in salaah, your complete pleasure (towards me) and (grant me) Your complete forgiveness.*

# Dua for goodness and protection from evil

رَبِّ اَسْاَلُكَ خَيْرَ مَا فِي هٰذَا الْيَوْمِ وَخَيْرَ مَا بَعْدَهُ وَاَعُوْذُ بِكَ مِنْ شَرِّ مَا فِي

هٰذَا الْيَوْمِ وَشَرِّ مَا بَعْدَهُ

*O Allah, I beg of You for all the good of this day as well as the coming days and I seek Your protection from all the evil of this day as well as the coming days.*

# Dua for Protection from laziness and Old Age

رَبِّ اَعُوْذُ بِكَ مِنَ الْكَسَلِ وَسُوْءِ الْكِبَرِ

*O Allah, I seek Your protection from laziness and the evil of old age.*

# Dua for protection from worry, grief, laziness, miserliness, cowardice, debt and oppression

اَللّٰهُمَّ اِنِّيْ اَعُوْذُ بِكَ مِنَ الْهَمِّ وَالْحُزْنِ، وَاَعُوْذُ بِكَ مِنَ الْعَجْزِ وَالْكَسَلِ

وَاَعُوْذُ بِكَ مِنَ الْجُبْنِ وَالْبُخْلِ وَاَعُوْذُ بِكَ مِنْ غَلَبَةِ الدَّيْنِ وَقَهْرِ الرِّجَالِ

*O Allah, I seek Your protection from worry and grief, I seek Your protection from weakness and laziness, from cowardice and miserliness and from being overpowered by debt and the oppression of men.*

# Dua to be pleased with the decision of Allah Ta'ala and to see Allah Ta'ala

اَللّٰهُمَّ اِنِّيْ اَسْأَلُكَ الرِّضَاءَ بَعْدَ الْقَضَاءِ، وَبَرْدَ الْعَيْشِ بَعْدَ الْمَوْتِ، وَلَذَّةَ النَّظَرِ اِلٰى وَجْهِكَ وَشَوْقًا اِلٰى لِقَائِكَ فِيْ غَيْرِ ضَرَّاءَ مُضِرَّةٍ وَّلَا فِتْنَةٍ مُّضِلَّةٍ

*O Allah, I beg You to make me pleased with Your decisions, (I beg You) a comfortable life after death, the extreme joy of seeing You and a passion for meeting You in a condition where I am not in any difficult position nor any fitnah (trial) that would make me misguided. I seek your protection from oppressing others or from being oppressed or that I should be unjust to anyone or others being unjust to me or that I should deliberately do an error or sin which You would not forgive.*

# Dua at the time of difficulty[1]

لَا اِلٰهَ اِلَّا اللهُ الْحَلِيْمُ الْكَرِيْمُ سُبْحَانَ اللهِ رَبِّ الْعَرْشِ الْعَظِيْمِ . اَلْحَمْدُ لِلّٰهِ رَبِّ الْعٰلَمِيْنَ ، اَسْأَلُكَ مُوْجِبَاتِ رَحْمَتِكَ وَعَزَائِمَ مَغْفِرَتِكَ وَالْعِصْمَةَ مِنْ كُلِّ ذَنْبٍ وَّالْغَنِيْمَةَ مِنْ كُلِّ بِرٍّ وَّالسَّلَامَةَ مِنْ كُلِّ اِثْمٍ ، لَا تَدَعْ لِيْ ذَنْبًا

---

[1] Hadhrat Abdullah ibn Abi Awfaa رَضِيَاللهُعَنْهُ narrates that Rasulullah صَلَّىاللهُعَلَيْهِوَسَلَّمَ once came out of his house and said, "Whoever has a need from Allah Ta'ala or from any person should perform wudhu in the best manner possible, perform two rakaats of salaah and then praise and glorify Allah Ta'ala, send durood upon me (i.e. Rasulullah صَلَّىاللهُعَلَيْهِوَسَلَّمَ) and read this dua.

اِلَّا غَفَرْتَهٗ، وَلَا هَمًّا اِلَّا فَرَّجْتَهٗ، وَلَا كَرْبًا اِلَّا نَفَّسْتَهٗ، وَلَا ضُرًّا اِلَّا كَشَفْتَهٗ،

وَلَا حَاجَةً هِيَ لَكَ رِضًا اِلَّا قَضَيْتَهَا يَا اَرْحَمَ الرَّاحِمِيْنَ

*There is no god besides Allah, The Most Tolerant and Generous, Who is free from any fault and The Rabb of the Great Throne (Arsh). Praise be to Allah, the master of the worlds. I ask You (O Allah) for all those things that will make Your mercy necessary on me, and all those things that will earn for me Your forgiveness. (I ask for) safety from sin, and I desire a full share of pious actions and complete safety from sins. (O Allah) let not a single sin of mine be left without it being forgiven, nor let any worry or pain be left from being relieved, nor let any grief be left from being removed, nor let any difficulty be left from being removed and nor any need of mine which You will be pleased with let it not be left from being completed. O The Most Merciful and Compassionate.*

# TUESDAY

## PRAISES OF ALLAH TA'ALA

سُبْحَانَكَ اللّٰهُمَّ وَبِحَمْدِكَ وَتَبَارَكَ اسْمُكَ وَتَعَالٰى جَدُّكَ وَلَاۤ اِلٰهَ غَيْرُكَ.

اَللّٰهُمَّ لَكَ الْحَمْدُ شُكْرًا وَّلَكَ الْمَنُّ فَضْلًا

*Glory be to You O Allah! Praise be to You, and blessed is Your name, very high is Your greatness, and there is no god besides You. O Allah, all praise is due to You with gratefulness and all kindness is due to You with grace.*

## DUROOD UPON RASULULLAH ﷺ

اَللّٰهُمَّ اَعْطِ مُحَمَّدَ الْوَسِيْلَةَ وَاجْعَلْ فِي الْمُصْطَفَيْنَ مَحَبَّتَهُ وَفِي الْاَعْلَيْنَ دَرَجَتَهُ وَفِي الْمُقَرَّبِيْنَ ذِكْرَهُ

*O Allah, Bless Nabi Muhammad ﷺ with the position of Waseelah (a special position in the aakhirat), fill his love into the hearts of the chosen ones, place him among the people of the highest rank and allow his name to be on the lips of those who are extremely close to You.*

## BEGGING ALLAH TA'ALA THROUGH HIS BEAUTIFUL NAMES

اَللّٰهُمَّ اِنِّيْ اَسْاَلُكَ بِاَنِّيْ اَشْهَدُ اَنَّكَ اَنْتَ اللّٰهُ لَا اِلٰهَ اِلَّا اَنْتَ الْاَحَدُ الصَّمَدُ الَّذِيْ لَمْ يَلِدْ وَلَمْ يُوْلَدْ وَلَمْ يَكُنْ لَّهُ كُفُوًا اَحَدٌ

*O Allah, I beg of You by saying that I bear witness that certainly You are Allah. There is no god besides You. You are One and totally not in need, Who was not born from anyone and did not give birth to anyone and there is no one equal to Him.*

## DUAS FOR AAFIYAH (GOOD CONDITIONS)[13]

اَللّٰهُمَّ اِنِّيْ اَسْاَلُكَ الْعَافِيَةَ

*O Allah, I beg of You for aafiyat (safety & ease).*

اَللّٰهُمَّ اِنِّيْ اَسْاَلُكَ الْعَافِيَةَ فِي الدُّنْيَا وَالْاٰخِرَةِ، اَللّٰهُمَّ اِنِّيْ اَسْاَلُكَ الْعَفْوَ وَالْعَافِيَةَ فِيْ دِيْنِيْ وَدُنْيَايَ وَاَهْلِيْ وَمَالِيْ

*O Allah, I beg of You for aafiyat (safety & ease) in this world and the Hereafter. O Allah, I beg of You for forgiveness and (aafiyat) safety in my Deen, my dunya, my family and in my wealth.*

اَللّٰهُمَّ اِنِّيْ اَسْاَلُكَ تَمَامَ الْعَافِيَةِ، وَاَسْاَلُكَ دَوَامَ الْعَافِيَةِ، وَاَسْاَلُكَ الشُّكْرَ عَلَى الْعَافِيَةِ

*O Allah, I beg of You for perfect and lasting ease and the ability to be grateful for it.*

---

[13] Rasulullah ﷺ has mentioned that the best thing a person can ask for is Aafiyah.

اَللّٰهُمَّ اِنِّيْ اَسْاَلُكَ الْعَافِيَةَ فِي الدُّنْيَا وَالْاٰخِرَةِ

*O Allah, I beg of You for aafiyat (safety & ease) in this world and the Hereafter.*

اَللّٰهُمَّ اِنِّيْ اَسْاَلُكَ الْعَفْوَ وَالْعَافِيَةَ فِيْ دِيْنِيْ وَدُنْيَايَ وَاَهْلِيْ وَمَالِيْ

*O Allah, I beg of Your forgiveness and aafiyat (safety) in my Deen, my dunya, my family, and in my wealth.*

اَللّٰهُمَّ عَافِنِيْ فِيْ بَدَنِيْ، اَللّٰهُمَّ عَافِنِيْ فِيْ سَمْعِيْ، اَللّٰهُمَّ عَافِنِيْ فِيْ بَصَرِيْ، لَا اِلٰهَ اِلَّا اَنْتَ (ثَلَاثَ مَرَّاتٍ)

*O Allah, grant me aafiyat (sound health) in my body, my hearing and my eye-sight. There is no god besides You. (Read thrice).*

## DUA FOR PROTECTION FROM AAFIYAH BEING TAKEN AWAY FROM US

اَللّٰهُمَّ اِنِّيْ اَعُوْذُ بِكَ مِنْ زَوَالِ نِعْمَتِكَ وَتَحَوُّلِ عَافِيَتِكَ وَفُجَاءَةِ نِقْمَتِكَ وَجَمِيْعِ سَخَطِكَ

*O Allah, I seek Your protection from losing Your favours and that Your aafiyat (complete protection) turns away from me and from sudden problems striking me and from all those things that will bring Your anger.*

## DUA FOR PURE RIZQ AND USING IT CORRECTLY

اَللّٰهُمَّ ارْزُقْنِيْ طَيِّبًا وَّاسْتَعْمِلْنِيْ طَيِّبًا

*O Allah, grant me pure sustenance and use me in good actions.*

## DUA FOR PURE HALAAL RIZQ

وَهَبْ لَنَا اَللّٰهُمَّ مِنْ رِّزْقِكَ الْحَلَالِ الطَّيِّبِ الْمُبَارَكِ مَا تَصُوْنُ بِهٖ وُجُوْهَنَا عَنِ التَّعَرُّضِ اِلٰى اَحَدٍ مِّنْ خَلْقِكَ، اَللّٰهُمَّ اجْعَلْ لَّنَا اِلَيْكَ طَرِيْقًا سَهْلًا مِّنْ غَيْرِ تَعَبٍ وَّلَا نَصَبٍ وَّلَا مِنَّةٍ وَّلَا تَبِعَةٍ، وَجَنِّبْنَا اللّٰهُمَّ الْحَرَامَ حَيْثُ كَانَ وَاَيْنَ كَانَ وَعِنْدَ مَنْ كَانَ

*O Allah, bless us with halaal sustenance which is pure and blessed, such that it will save our respect from having to come to any one of Your creation for help. O Allah, make for us an easy path towards You which is not tiring or painful and in which we will not owe anything to others. O Allah, save us from haraam (unlawful) in whichever form, from whichever place or from any person.*

## DUA FOR INCREASE AND BARKAT IN ONES RIZQ

اَللّٰهُمَّ اغْفِرْ لِيْ ذَنْبِيْ وَوَسِّعْ لِيْ فِيْ دَارِيْ وَبَارِكْ لِيْ فِيْ رِزْقِيْ

*O Allah, forgive my sins, grant me spaciousness in my home and bless me*

*with barakah (blessings) in my sustenance.*

## Dua for protection from pride caused by wealth

اَللّٰهُمَّ اِنِّيْ اَعُوْذُبِكَ مِنْ بَطَرِ الْغِنٰى وَمَذَلَّةِ الْفَقْرِ

*O Allah, I seek Your protection from pride because of wealth and disgrace due to poverty.*

## Dua for Pure Sustenance, Beneficial Knowledge and Accepted Deeds

اَللّٰهُمَّ اِنِّيْ اَسْاَلُكَ رِزْقًا طَيِّبًا وَّعِلْمًا نَّافِعًا وَّعَمَلًا مُّتَقَبَّلًا

*O Allah, I beg You for Halaal (pure) sustenance, beneficial knowledge and deeds that are accepted.*

## Dua for Contentment

اَللّٰهُمَّ قَنِّعْنِيْ بِمَا رَزَقْتَنِيْ، وَبَارِكْ لِيْ فِيْهِ، وَاخْلُفْ عَلٰى كُلِّ غَائِبَةٍ لِّيْ بِخَيْرٍ

*O Allah, make me content with whatever You have provided for me and give me barakah (blessings) in it and be a Protector on behalf of me over that which is not in front of me (i.e. my family and wealth).*

# DUA FOR TAWAKKUL, HIDAAYAT AND HELP

اَللّٰهُمَّ اجْعَلْنِيْ مِمَّنْ تَوَكَّلَ عَلَيْكَ فَكَفَيْتَهُ، وَاسْتَهْدَاكَ فَهَدَيْتَهُ، وَاسْتَنْصَرَكَ فَنَصَرْتَهُ

*O Allah, make me from amongst those who placed their trust in You and then found You to be sufficient. (Make me from those) who sought guidance from You and were then guided and (make me from those) who asked You for help and then You helped them.*

## DUA FOR ABILITY TO DO GOOD ACTIONS

اَللّٰهُمَّ وَفِّقْنِيْ لِمَا تُحِبُّ وَتَرْضٰى مِنَ الْقَوْلِ وَالْعَمَلِ وَالْفِعْلِ وَالنِّيَّةِ وَالْهُدٰى اِنَّكَ عَلٰى كُلِّ شَيْءٍ قَدِيْرٌ

*O Allah, bless me with the taufeeq (ability) to do all such words, deeds, actions, intentions and acts of guidance that will lead to Your pleasure and happiness. Certainly You have power over everything.*

## DUA TO BE IN THE COMPANY OF THE AMBIYAA عَلَيْهِمُ السَّلَام

اَللّٰهُمَّ اِنِّيْ اَسْأَلُكَ ثَوَابَ الشَّاكِرِيْنَ وَنُزُلَ الْمُقَرَّبِيْنَ وَمُرَافَقَةَ النَّبِيِّيْنَ وَيَقِيْنَ الصِّدِّيْقِيْنَ وَذِلَّةَ الْمُتَّقِيْنَ وَاِخْبَاتَ الْمُوْقِنِيْنَ حَتّٰى تَوَفَّانِيْ عَلٰى ذٰلِكَ يَا اَرْحَمَ الرَّاحِمِيْنَ

*O Allah, I ask of You to bless me with the reward of the Shaakireen (Those who are grateful to You), the respect granted to those who are very close to You, the company of the Ambiyaa عَلَيْهِمُ السَّلَام, the yaqeen (conviction) of the truthful, the humility of the pious and the submission of those who have Yaqeen. O The Most Merciful and Compassionate, bless me with all of this till my death.*

## DUA FOR PROTECTION FROM AN EVIL SPOUSE, AN EVIL CHILD, EVIL WEALTH AND CUNNING FRIENDS

اَللّٰهُمَّ اِنِّيْ اَعُوْذُ بِكَ مِنِ امْرَاَةٍ تُشَيِّبُنِيْ قَبْلَ الْمَشِيْبِ وَاَعُوْذُ بِكَ مِنْ وَّلَدٍ يَّكُوْنُ عَلَيَّ وَبَالًا وَاَعُوْذُ بِكَ مِنْ مَّالٍ يَّكُوْنُ عَلَيَّ عَذَابًا وَاَعُوْذُ بِكَ مِنْ صَاحِبٍ خَدِيْعَةٍ اِنْ رَّاٰى حَسَنَةً دَفَنَهَا وَاِنْ رَّاٰى سَيِّئَةً اَفْشَاهَا .

*O Allah! I seek Your protection from a wife who makes me old before my time, from children who become a nuisance to me, from wealth which becomes a punishment for me and from a disloyal friend who conceals my good and discloses my faults far and wide.*

# WEDNESDAY

## PRAISES OF ALLAH TA'ALA

اَللّٰهُمَّ لَكَ الْحَمْدُ كُلُّهُ، وَلَكَ الشُّكْرُ كُلُّهُ، وَلَكَ الْمُلْكُ كُلُّهُ، وَلَكَ الْخَلْقُ كُلُّهُ، بِيَدِكَ الْخَيْرُ كُلُّهُ، وَاِلَيْكَ يَرْجِعُ الْاَمْرُكُلُّهُ،

*O Allah, all praise and thanks is for You, the entire kingdom and creation belong to You. All good is in Your hands and all matters return to You.*

## DUROOD UPON RASULULLAH ﷺ

جَزَى اللهُ عَنَّا مُحَمَّدًا صَلَّى اللهُ عَلَيْهِ وَسَلَّمَ بِمَا هُوَ اَهْلُهُ

*O Allah, grant our Noble Master Hadhrat Muhammad ﷺ a suitable reward on our behalf*

## BEGGING ALLAH TA'ALA THROUGH HIS BEAUTIFUL NAMES

اَللّٰهُمَّ اِنِّيْ اَسْاَلُكَ بِاَنَّ لَكَ الْحَمْدَ لَا اِلٰهَ اِلَّا اَنْتَ (وَحْدَكَ لَا شَرِيْكَ لَكَ) الْحَنَّانُ الْمَنَّانُ بَدِيْعُ السَّمٰوَاتِ وَالْاَرْضِ يَاذَا الْجَلَالِ وَالْاِكْرَامِ يَا حَيُّ يَا قَيُّوْمُ . يَا اَرْحَمَ الرَّاحِمِيْنَ

*O Allah, I beg You by saying that all praise is for You. There is no god besides You. You are One, You have no partner. You are Most Kind and*

*Most Compassionate, The Creator of the heavens and the earth. O, You Majestic and Generous Rabb, The Everlasting, The Sustainer, O, The Most Merciful of those who show mercy.*

## DUA FOR GOOD AKHLAAQ (CHARACTER)

اَللّٰهُمَّ اهْدِنِيْ لِاَحْسَنِ الْاَخْلَاقِ لَا يَهْدِيْ لِاَحْسَنِهَا اِلَّا اَنْتَ وَاصْرِفْ عَنِّيْ سَيِّئَهَا لَا يَصْرِفُ عَنِّيْ سَيِّئَهَا اِلَّا اَنْتَ

*O Allah, grant me excellent character as You alone can guide me to it and remove from me all evil character which You alone can remove.*

## DUA FOR PROTECTION FROM EVIL CHARACTER, EVIL ACTIONS, EVIL DESIRES AND DREADFUL DISEASES

اَللّٰهُمَّ اِنِّيْ اَعُوْذُبِكَ مِنْ مُنْكَرَاتِ الْاَخْلَاقِ وَالْاَعْمَالِ وَالْاَهْوَاءِ وَالْاَدْوَاءِ

*O Allah, I seek Your protection from bad manners, evil actions, evil desires and dreadful diseases.*

## DUA FOR PROTECTION FROM FIGHTS, HYPOCRISY AND EVIL CHARACTER

اَللّٰهُمَّ اِنِّيْ اَعُوْذُبِكَ مِنَ الشِّقَاقِ وَالنِّفَاقِ وَسُوْءِ الْاَخْلَاقِ

*O Allah, I seek Your protection from causing disunity (fights), from hypocrisy and from bad manners.*

## DUA FOR THE LOVE OF ALLAH TA'ALA, EARNING OF RESPECT AND PROTECTION FROM EVIL CHARACTER

اِلَيْكَ رَبِّ فَحَبِّبْنِي، وَفِي نَفْسِي لَكَ رَبِّ فَذَلِّلْنِي، وَفِي اَعْيُنِ النَّاسِ فَعَظِّمْنِي، وَمِنْ سَيِّئِ الْاَخْلَاقِ فَجَنِّبْنِي

*O Allah, make me beloved to You, place in my heart submission (humility) towards You and give me honour in the eyes of the people and save me from evil manners.*

## DUA FOR GENEROSITY, PURE SUSTENANCE AND CONTENTMENT (SATISFACTION)

اَللّٰهُمَّ اغْفِرْ لِي ذَنْبِي وَوَسِّعْ لِي خُلُقِي وَطَيِّبْ لِي كَسْبِي وَقَنِّعْنِي بِمَا رَزَقْتَنِي وَلَا تُذْهِبْ طَلَبِي اِلٰى شَيْءٍ صَرَّفْتَهٗ عَنِّي

*O Allah, forgive my sins, increase my character (make me generous), bless me with halaal sustenance, give me contentment in my earnings and don't make me wish for something which You have not written for me.*

## DUA FOR GOOD CHARACTER

اَللّٰهُمَّ اَحْسَنْتَ خَلْقِي فَاَحْسِنْ خُلُقِي

*O Allah, You have given me a good body. So (please) bless me with good manners as well.*

## Dua for Good Health, Purity, Trustworthiness and Good Character

اَللّٰهُمَّ اِنِّيْ اَسْـَٔلُكَ الصِّحَّةَ وَالْعِفَّةَ وَالْاَمَانَةَ وَحُسْنَ الْخُلُقِ وَالرِّضَا بِالْقَدَرِ

*O Allah, I beg You for good health, purity, trustworthiness, good manners and to be happy with Your taqdeer.*

## Dua for Guidance

اَللّٰهُمَّ خِرْ لِيْ وَاخْتَرْ لِيْ

*O Allah, You choose for me what is best for me and then give it to me.*

## Dua for Guidance and Being a Means of Guidance to Others

اَللّٰهُمَّ اجْعَلْنَا هَادِيْنَ مُهْتَدِيْنَ غَيْرَ ضَالِّيْنَ وَلَا مُضِلِّيْنَ، سِلْمًا لِاَوْلِيَائِكَ وَحَرْبًا لِاَعْدَآئِكَ، نُحِبُّ بِحُبِّكَ مَنْ اَحَبَّكَ، وَنُعَادِيْ بِعَدَاوَتِكَ مَنْ خَالَفَكَ مِنْ خَلْقِكَ

*O Allah, make us from those who are rightly guided and from those who guide others. Not from those who are misguided and those who misguide others. (Make us) from those who make peace with Your friends and are always at war with Your enemies, who love those that love You only because of love for You and those who show hatred because of your hatred towards Your enemies from Your creation.*

## DUA FOR PROTECTION OF WHATEVER GOOD HAS BEEN GIVEN TO US

اَللّٰهُمَّ لَا تَكِلْنِيْ اِلٰى نَفْسِيْ طَرْفَةَ عَيْنٍ وَّلَا تَنْزِعْ مِنِّيْ صَالِحَ مَا اَعْطَيْتَنِيْ

*O Allah, do not leave me to myself for the blinking of an eye and do not take away any good which You have already give to me.*

## BEGGING ALLAH TA'ALA TO TAKE CHARGE OF ALL OUR WORKS

اَللّٰهُمَّ اِنَّ قُلُوْبَنَا وَنَوَاصِيَنَا وَجَوَارِحَنَا بِيَدِكَ لَمْ تُمَلِّكْنَا مِنْهَا شَيْئًا فَاِذَا فَعَلْتَ ذٰلِكَ بِنَا فَكُنْ اَنْتَ وَلِيَّنَا وَاهْدِنَا اِلٰى سَوَاءِ السَّبِيْلِ

*O Allah, our hearts, foreheads and limbs are in Your control. You did not make us the owners of any of these things. Since You have decide it in this way, then be our guardian and guide us to the straight path.*

## DUA FOR GUIDANCE, TAQWA AND FORGIVENESS

اَللّٰهُمَّ اهْدِنِيْ بِالْهُدٰى ، وَنَقِّنِيْ بِالتَّقْوٰى ، وَاغْفِرْ لِيْ فِي الْاٰخِرَةِ وَالْاُوْلٰى

*O Allah guide me with (Your) guidance, cleanse me with taqwa (piety) and*

*forgive me in this life and the hereafter.*

## DUA FOR TAQWA AND PURITY

رَبِّ اَعْطِ نَفْسِيْ تَقْوٰهَا وَزَكِّهَا اَنْتَ خَيْرُ مَنْ زَكّٰهَا اَنْتَ وَلِيُّهَا وَمَوْلٰهَا

*O Allah, bless me with taqwa (Your fear) and purify my soul as You are the Best Purifier. You are the Guardian and Master of my soul.*

## BEGGING ALLAH TA'ALA TO POUR HIS MERCY UPON US

اَللّٰهُمَّ افْتَحْ اَقْفَالَ قُلُوْبِنَا بِذِكْرِكَ ، وَاَتْمِمْ عَلَيْنَا بِنِعْمَتِكَ ، وَاَسْبِغْ عَلَيْنَا مِنْ فَضْلِكَ ، وَاجْعَلْنَا مِنْ عِبَادِكَ الصَّالِحِيْنَ

*O Allah, open up the locks of our hearts with Your remembrance, complete Your favour upon us, pour Your grace over us and make us Your pious servants.*

## DUA FOR PROTECTION AGAINST JAHANNAM, PUNISHMENT IN THE GRAVE, DAJJAAL, SINS AND DEBT

اَللّٰهُمَّ اِنِّيْ اَعُوْذُبِكَ مِنْ عَذَابِ جَهَنَّمَ ، وَاَعُوْذُبِكَ مِنْ عَذَابِ الْقَبْرِ ، وَاَعُوْذُبِكَ مِنْ فِتْنَةِ الْمَسِيْحِ الدَّجَّالِ ، وَاَعُوْذُبِكَ مِنْ فِتْنَةِ الْمَحْيَا وَالْمَمَاتِ وَاَعُوْذُبِكَ مِنَ الْمَأْثَمِ وَالْمَغْرَمِ

*O Allah, I seek Your protection from the punishment of jahannam, the punishment of the grave, from the mischief of Dajjaal, from the tests of life and death, from sins and from debts.*

## DUA FOR PROTECTION FROM SHAMELESS ACTIONS

اَللّٰهُمَّ حَصِّنْ فَرْجِيْ، وَيَسِّرْ لِيْ اَمْرِيْ

*O Allah, guard my private parts and make my work easy for me.*

## DUA FOR PROTECTION FROM SHIRK AND SHOW

اَللّٰهُمَّ اِنِّيْ اَعُوْذُبِكَ مِنْ اَنْ اُشْرِكَ بِكَ شَيْئًا وَّاَنَا اَعْلَمُ بِهٖ وَاَسْتَغْفِرُكَ لِمَا لَا اَعْلَمُ بِهٖ

*O Allah, I seek Your protection from joining any partners with You knowingly and I beg Your forgiveness for all that I have done unknowingly.*

سُبْحٰنَكَ اللّٰهُمَّ وَتَحِيَّتُهُمْ فِيْهَا سَلٰمٌ وَاٰخِرُ دَعْوٰهُمْ اَنِ الْحَمْدُ لِلّٰهِ رَبِّ الْعٰلَمِيْنَ

*O Allah, You are free from all blemishes. The greeting of the inmates of Jannah will be: "Salaam" and their final call will be: "All praise is due to Allah the Nourisher of the worlds."*

# THURSDAY

## PRAISES OF ALLAH TA'ALA

اَللّٰهُمَّ لَكَ الْحَمْدُ اَنْتَ قَيِّمُ السَّمٰوَاتِ وَالْاَرْضِ وَمَنْ فِيْهِنَّ وَلَكَ الْحَمْدُ اَنْتَ مَلِكُ السَّمٰوَاتِ وَالْاَرْضِ وَمَنْ فِيْهِنَّ وَلَكَ الْحَمْدُ اَنْتَ نُوْرُ السَّمٰوَاتِ وَالْاَرْضِ وَمَنْ فِيْهِنَّ وَلَكَ الْحَمْدُ اَنْتَ الْحَقُّ وَوَعْدُكَ الْحَقُّ وَلِقَآؤُكَ حَقٌّ وَقَوْلُكَ حَقٌّ وَالْجَنَّةُ حَقٌّ وَالنَّارُ حَقٌّ وَالنَّبِيُّوْنَ حَقٌّ وَمُحَمَّدٌ صَلَّى اللهُ عَلَيْهِ وَسَلَّمَ رَسُوْلُ اللهِ حَقٌّ وَالسَّاعَةُ حَقٌّ

*O Allah, all praise is for You and You are the Controller of the heavens and the earth and whatever is in them. You are the Ruler of the heavens and the earth and whatever is in them. All praise is for You. You are the (noor) light of the heavens and the earth and whatever is in them. All praise is for You. You are True, Your promise is true and our meeting You is a reality, Your word is true. Paradise is a reality. Hell is a reality and all the Ambiyaa are true. Muhammad ﷺ, the Messenger of Allah, is true and the Hour (of Qiyamat) is a reality.*

## DUROOD UPON RASULULLAH ﷺ

اَللّٰهُمَّ صَلِّ عَلَى (سَيِّدِنَا) مُحَمَّدٍ عَبْدِكَ وَرَسُوْلِكَ وَصَلِّ عَلَى الْمُؤْمِنِيْنَ وَالْمُؤْمِنَاتِ وَالْمُسْلِمِيْنَ وَالْمُسْلِمَاتِ

*O Allah, send salutations upon Nabi Muhammad ﷺ, Your servant and Your messenger and send peace upon all the believing men and women.*

## BEGGING ALLAH TA'ALA THROUGH HIS BEAUTIFUL NAMES

يَا وَاسِعَ الْمَغْفِرَةِ، يَا بَاسِطَ الْيَدَيْنِ بِالرَّحْمَةِ

*O' The One with everlasting forgiveness, The One with both hands stretched out with mercy.*

## DUA FOR BLESSINGS AT THE TIME OF DEATH AND AFTER DEATH (RECITE 25 TIMES DAILY)[14]

اَللّٰهُمَّ بَارِكْ لِيْ فِي الْمَوْتِ وَفِيْمَا بَعْدَ الْمَوْتِ

*O Allah, bless me at the time of my death and (bless me) in what follows after death.*

## DUA FOR PROTECTION FROM A BAD DEATH

اَللّٰهُمَّ اِنِّيْ اَعُوْذُبِكَ مِنْ مَّوْتِ الْهَمِّ، وَاَعُوْذُبِكَ مِنْ مَّوْتِ الْغَمِّ

*O Allah, I seek Your protection from death in a state of worry. And I seek your protection from death in a state of grief.*

---

[14] One who recites this dua 25 times daily will attain the rank of the *Shuhadaaa* (Martyrs)

# DUA FOR PROTECTION FROM SUDDEN DEATH, SNAKE BITES, WILD ANIMALS, DROWNING AND BURNING

اَللّٰهُمَّ اِنِّيْ اَعُوْذُبِكَ مِنْ مَوْتِ الْفُجَاءَةِ وَمِنْ لَّدْغَةِ الْحَيَّةِ وَمِنَ السَّبُعِ وَمِنَ الْغَرَقِ وَمِنَ الْحَرَقِ وَمِنْ اَنْ اَخِرَّ عَلٰى شَيْءٍ وَمِنَ الْقَتْلِ عِنْدَ فِرَارِ الزَّحْفِ

*O Allah, I seek Your protection from sudden death, from being bitten by a snake, or being attacked by a wild animal, from being drowned or burnt to death, or that I should fall down upon anything and from being killed whilst I'm running away from the battle field.*

## DUA FOR HELP AT THE TIME OF DEATH

اَللّٰهُمَّ اَعِنِّيْ عَلٰى غَمَرَاتِ الْمَوْتِ وَسَكَرَاتِ الْمَوْتِ

*O Allah, please help me during the difficulties and pains of death.*

## DUA FOR PROTECTION FROM ALL EVILS

اَللّٰهُمَّ رَبَّ السَّمٰوَاتِ السَّبْعِ وَمَا اَظَلَّتْ وَرَبَّ الْاَرَضِيْنَ وَمَا اَقَلَّتْ وَرَبَّ الشَّيَاطِيْنِ وَمَا اَضَلَّتْ كُنْ لِّيْ جَارًا مِّنْ شَرِّ خَلْقِكَ اَجْمَعِيْنَ اَنْ يَّفْرُطَ عَلَيَّ اَحَدٌ مِّنْهُمْ اَوْ اَنْ يَّطْغٰى عَزَّ جَارُكَ وَتَبَارَكَ اسْمُكَ.

*O Allah! The Rabb of the seven heavens and whatever it over-shadows, the Rabb of the earths and whatever it holds, the Rabb of the devils and what ever evil they had spread, be a Protector for me against the evil of all Your creatures if they be unjust or cruel to me. Your protection is indeed strong and Your name is full of blessings.*

## DUA FOR EASE AT THE TIME OF DEATH

حَسْبِيَ اللّٰهُ عِنْدَ الْمَوْتِ

*Allah Ta'ala is enough for me during the pains of death.*

## DUAS FOR PROTECTION

اَللّٰهُمَّ اِنَّا نَجْعَلُكَ فِيْ نُحُوْرِهِمْ ، وَنَعُوْذُ بِكَ مِنْ شُرُوْرِهِمْ

*O Allah, we place You in front of us when fighting them and seek Your protection against their evil plans.*

اَللّٰهُمَّ وَاقِيَةً كَوَاقِيَةِ الْوَلِيْدِ

*O Allah, grant me protection like the protection given to a new born baby.*

اَللّٰهُمَّ اسْتُرْ عَوْرَاتِيْ وَاٰمِنْ رَوْعَاتِيْ

*O Allah, hide my faults and save me from fear.*

## DUA FOR PROTECTION FROM ALL SIDES

اَللّٰهُمَّ احْفَظْنِيْ مِنْ بَيْنِ يَدَيَّ وَمِنْ خَلْفِيْ وَعَنْ يَّمِيْنِيْ وَعَنْ شِمَالِيْ وَمِنْ فَوْقِيْ وَاَعُوْذُ بِعَظَمَتِكَ اَنْ اُغْتَالَ مِنْ تَحْتِيْ رَضِيْنَا بِاللّٰهِ رَبًّا وَّبِالْاِسْلَامِ دِيْنًا وَّبِمُحَمَّدٍ صَلَّى اللّٰهُ عَلَيْهِ وَسَلَّمَ رَسُوْلًا وَّنَبِيًّا

*O Allah, protect me from in front of me and from behind me, on my right and on my left and above me. I seek protection in Your Greatness that I may be destroyed by any disaster from beneath me. We are pleased with Allah as our Rabb, Islam as our religion and Hadhrat Muhammad ﷺ as our Rasul and Messenger.*

## DUA TO BE BLESSED WITH THE HOLY QUR-AAN

اَللّٰهُمَّ ارْحَمْنِيْ بِالْقُرْاٰنِ الْعَظِيْمِ ، وَاجْعَلْهُ لِيْ اِمَامًا وَّنُوْرًا وَّهُدًى وَّرَحْمَةً . اَللّٰهُمَّ ذَكِّرْنِيْ مِنْهُ مَا نَسِيْتُ ، وَعَلِّمْنِيْ مِنْهُ مَا جَهِلْتُ ، وَارْزُقْنِيْ تِلَاوَتَهُ اٰنَاءَ اللَّيْلِ وَاٰنَاءَ النَّهَارِ ، وَاجْعَلْهُ لِيْ حُجَّةً يَّا رَبَّ الْعَالَمِيْنَ

*O Allah, have mercy on me through the blessings of the Holy Qur-aan and make it a guide for me, a means of light, a means of guidance and a means of mercy as well. O Allah, make me remember what I have forgotten of the Holy Qur-aan, and give me an understanding of those parts which I am ignorant of. Cause me to read it during the hours of the night and day and make it a proof for me, O Rabb of the worlds.*

## DUA FOR FORGIVENESS OF THE ENTIRE UMMAH

اَللّٰهُمَّ اغْفِرْ لِيْ وَلِلْمُؤْمِنِيْنَ وَالْمُؤْمِنَاتِ وَالْمُسْلِمِيْنَ وَالْمُسْلِمَاتِ ، وَاَلِّفْ بَيْنَ قُلُوْبِهِمْ ، وَاَصْلِحْ ذَاتَ بَيْنِهِمْ وَانْصُرْهُمْ عَلٰى عَدُوِّكَ وَعَدُوِّهِمْ

*O Allah, forgive me and all the believing men and women, all the Muslim men and women, join their hearts, correct their mutual works and help them against Your enemy and their enemy.*

## DUA FOR BECOMING SINCERE FRIENDS OF ALLAH TA'ALA

اَللّٰهُمَّ اجْعَلْنَا سَامِعِيْنَ مُطِيْعِيْنَ وَاَوْلِيَاءَ مُخْلِصِيْنَ وَرُفَقَاءَ مُصَاحِبِيْنَ ، اَللّٰهُمَّ اَبْلِغْهُ مِنَّا السَّلَامَ ، وَارْدُدْ عَلَيْنَا مِنْهُ السَّلَامِ

*O Allah, make us those who will listen and obey Your commands and make us sincere friends and good companions. O Allah send our salaams to Rasulullah ﷺ and bless us with a salaam from him.*

## DUA TO BE IN THE COMPANY OF RASULULLAH ﷺ

اَللّٰهُمَّ اجْعَلْ نَبِيَّنَا لَنَا فَرَطًا وَحَوْضَهُ لَنَا مَوْرِدًا . اَللّٰهُمَّ احْشُرْنَا فِيْ زُمْرَتِهِ ، وَاسْتَعْمِلْنَا بِسُنَّتِهِ ، وَتَوَفَّنَا عَلٰى مِلَّتِهِ ، وَاجْعَلْنَا فِيْ زُمْرَتِهِ وَحِزْبِهِ

*O Allah, make our Nabi ﷺ our guide and make his pond (Haudh-e-Kausar) a place for quenching our thirst. O Allah, raise us (on the Day of*

*Qiyaamah) from His group, allow us to follow His Sunnah, cause us to die on His ways and make us from amongst His group.*

## DUA FOR PROTECTION FROM LAZINESS AND OLD AGE

رَبِّ اَعُوْذُبِكَ مِنَ الْكَسَلِ وَسُوْءِ الْكِبَرِ

*O Allah, I seek Your protection from laziness and extreme old age*

## DUA FOR PROTECTION FROM WORRY, GRIEF, LAZINESS, MISERLINESS AND DEBT

اَللّٰهُمَّ اِنِّیْ اَعُوْذُبِكَ مِنَ الْهَمِّ وَالْحُزْنِ ، وَاَعُوْذُبِكَ مِنَ الْعَجْزِ وَالْكَسَلِ وَاَعُوْذُبِكَ مِنَ الْجُبْنِ وَالْبُخْلِ وَاَعُوْذُبِكَ مِنْ غَلَبَةِ الدَّيْنِ وَقَهْرِ الرِّجَالِ

*O Allah, I seek Your protection from worry and grief, I seek Your protection from weakness and laziness, from cowardice and miserliness and from being overpowered by debt and oppression of men.*

## CONCLUDING DUA

اَللّٰهُمَّ هٰذَا الدُّعَاءُ وَعَلَيْكَ الْاِجَابَةُ ، وَهٰذَا الْجُهْدُ وَعَلَيْكَ التُّكْلَانُ

*O Allah, making dua is our duty and accepting our duas is Your promise. We make the effort but our total reliance is on You.*

سُبْحٰنَ رَبِّكَ رَبِّ الْعِزَّةِ عَمَّا يَصِفُوْنَ وَسَلٰمٌ عَلَى الْمُرْسَلِيْنَ، وَالْحَمْدُ لِلّٰهِ رَبِّ الْعٰلَمِيْنَ

*Glorified is Your Rabb, The Rabb of Honour and Power. He is free from what the unbelievers say about Him. Peace be upon the Messengers and all praise is due to Allah, the Master of the worlds.*

## *FRIDAY*

سَلَامٌ عَلَى عِبَادِهِ الَّذِيْنَ اصْطَفَى ، سَلَامٌ عَلَى الْمُرْسَلِيْنَ

(١) أَللّٰهُمَّ صَلِّ عَلَى (سَيِّدِنَا وَ مَوْلَانَا) مُحَمَّدٍ وَّ عَلَى اٰلِ (سَيِّدِنَا وَ مَوْلَانَا) مُحَمَّدٍ وَّ أَنْزِلْهُ الْمَقْعَدَ الْمُقَرَّبَ عِنْدَكَ.

(٢) أَللّٰهُمَّ رَبَّ هٰذِهِ الدَّعْوَةِ الْقَائِمَةِ وَالصَّلٰوةِ النَّافِعَةِ صَلِّ عَلَى (سَيِّدِنَا وَ مَوْلَانَا) مُحَمَّدٍ وَّارْضَ عَنِّيْ رِضًا لَّا تَسْخَطْ بَعْدَهُ اَبَدًا.

(٣) أَللّٰهُمَّ صَلِّ عَلَى (سَيِّدِنَا وَ مَوْلَانَا) مُحَمَّدٍ عَبْدِكَ وَ رَسُوْلِكَ وَ صَلِّ عَلَى الْمُؤْمِنِيْنَ وَ الْمُؤْمِنَاتِ وَ الْمُسْلِمِيْنَ وَ الْمُسْلِمَاتِ.

(٤) أَللّٰهُمَّ صَلِّ عَلَى (سَيِّدِنَا وَ مَوْلَانَا) مُحَمَّدٍ وَّ عَلَى اٰلِ (سَيِّدِنَا وَ مَوْلَانَا) مُحَمَّدٍ وَّ بَارِكْ عَلَى (سَيِّدِنَا وَ مَوْلَانَا) مُحَمَّدٍ وَّ عَلَى اٰلِ (سَيِّدِنَا وَ مَوْلَانَا) مُحَمَّدٍ وَّ ارْحَمْ (سَيِّدِنَا وَ مَوْلَانَا) مُحَمَّدًا وَّ اٰلَ (سَيِّدِنَا وَ مَوْلَانَا) مُحَمَّدٍ كَمَا صَلَّيْتَ وَ بَارَكْتَ وَ رَحِمْتَ عَلَى (سَيِّدِنَا) إِبْرَاهِيْمَ وَ عَلَى اٰلِ (سَيِّدِنَا) إِبْرَاهِيْمَ إِنَّكَ حَمِيْدٌ مَجِيْدٌ.

۵ اَللّٰهُمَّ صَلِّ عَلٰى (سَيِّدِنَا وَ مَوْلَانَا) مُحَمَّدٍ وَّ عَلٰى اٰلِ (سَيِّدِنَا وَ مَوْلَانَا) مُحَمَّدٍ كَمَا صَلَّيْتَ عَلٰى اٰلِ (سَيِّدِنَا) إِبْرَاهِيْمَ إِنَّكَ حَمِيْدٌ مَّجِيْدٌ، اَللّٰهُمَّ بَارِكْ عَلٰى (سَيِّدِنَا وَ مَوْلَانَا) مُحَمَّدٍ وَّ عَلٰى اٰلِ (سَيِّدِنَا وَ مَوْلَانَا) مُحَمَّدٍ كَمَا بَارَكْتَ عَلٰى اٰلِ (سَيِّدِنَا) إِبْرَاهِيْمَ إِنَّكَ حَمِيْدٌ مَّجِيْدٌ.

۶ اَللّٰهُمَّ صَلِّ عَلٰى (سَيِّدِنَا وَ مَوْلَانَا) مُحَمَّدٍ وَّ عَلٰى اٰلِ (سَيِّدِنَا وَ مَوْلَانَا) مُحَمَّدٍ كَمَا صَلَّيْتَ عَلٰى اٰلِ (سَيِّدِنَا) إِبْرَاهِيْمَ اِنَّكَ حَمِيْدٌ مَّجِيْدٌ وَ بَارِكْ عَلٰى (سَيِّدِنَا وَ مَوْلَانَا) مُحَمَّدٍ وَّ عَلٰى اٰلِ (سَيِّدِنَا وَ مَوْلَانَا) مُحَمَّدٍ كَمَا بَارَكْتَ عَلٰى اٰلِ (سَيِّدِنَا) إِبْرَاهِيْمَ إِنَّكَ حَمِيْدٌ مَّجِيْدٌ.

۷ اَللّٰهُمَّ صَلِّ عَلٰى (سَيِّدِنَا وَ مَوْلَانَا) مُحَمَّدٍ وَّ عَلٰى اٰلِ (سَيِّدِنَا وَ مَوْلَانَا) مُحَمَّدٍ كَمَا صَلَّيْتَ عَلٰى (سَيِّدِنَا) اِبْرَاهِيْمَ اِنَّكَ حَمِيْدٌ مَّجِيْدٌ اَللّٰهُمَّ بَارِكْ عَلٰى (سَيِّدِنَا وَ مَوْلَانَا) مُحَمَّدٍ وَّ عَلٰى اٰلِ (سَيِّدِنَا وَ مَوْلَانَا) مُحَمَّدٍ كَمَا بَارَكْتَ عَلٰى (سَيِّدِنَا) اِبْرَاهِيْمَ اِنَّكَ حَمِيْدٌ مَّجِيْدٌ.

۸ اَللّٰهُمَّ صَلِّ عَلٰى (سَيِّدِنَا وَ مَوْلَانَا) مُحَمَّدٍ وَّ عَلٰى اٰلِ (سَيِّدِنَا وَ مَوْلَانَا) مُحَمَّدٍ كَمَا صَلَّيْتَ عَلٰى (سَيِّدِنَا) اِبْرَاهِيْمَ وَ عَلٰى اٰلِ (سَيِّدِنَا) اِبْرَاهِيْمَ اِنَّكَ

حَمِيدٌ مَّجِيدٌ وَ بَارِكْ عَلٰى (سَيِّدِنَا وَ مَوْلَانَا) مُحَمَّدٍ وَّ عَلٰى اٰلِ (سَيِّدِنَا وَ مَوْلَانَا) مُحَمَّدٍ كَمَا بَارَكْتَ عَلٰى (سَيِّدِنَا) إِبْرَاهِيْمَ اِنَّكَ حَمِيدٌ مَّجِيدٌ.

۹ اَللّٰهُمَّ صَلِّ عَلٰى (سَيِّدِنَا وَ مَوْلَانَا) مُحَمَّدٍ وَّ عَلٰى اٰلِ (سَيِّدِنَا وَ مَوْلَانَا) مُحَمَّدٍ كَمَا صَلَّيْتَ عَلٰى (سَيِّدِنَا) اِبْرَاهِيْمَ وَ بَارِكْ عَلٰى (سَيِّدِنَا وَ مَوْلَانَا) مُحَمَّدٍ وَّ عَلٰى اٰلِ (سَيِّدِنَا وَ مَوْلَانَا) مُحَمَّدٍ كَمَا بَارَكْتَ عَلٰى (سَيِّدِنَا) اِبْرَاهِيْمَ اِنَّكَ حَمِيدٌ مَّجِيدٌ.

۱۰ اَللّٰهُمَّ صَلِّ عَلٰى (سَيِّدِنَا وَ مَوْلَانَا) مُحَمَّدٍ وَّ عَلٰى اٰلِ (سَيِّدِنَا وَ مَوْلَانَا) مُحَمَّدٍ كَمَا صَلَّيْتَ عَلٰى (سَيِّدِنَا) اِبْرَاهِيْمَ اِنَّكَ حَمِيدٌ مَّجِيدٌ اَللّٰهُمَّ بَارِكْ عَلٰى (سَيِّدِنَا وَ مَوْلَانَا) مُحَمَّدٍ وَّ عَلٰى اٰلِ (سَيِّدِنَا وَ مَوْلَانَا) مُحَمَّدٍ كَمَا بَارَكْتَ عَلٰى اٰلِ (سَيِّدِنَا) اِبْرَاهِيْمَ اِنَّكَ حَمِيدٌ مَّجِيدٌ.

۱۱ اَللّٰهُمَّ صَلِّ عَلٰى (سَيِّدِنَا وَ مَوْلَانَا) مُحَمَّدٍ وَّ عَلٰى اٰلِ (سَيِّدِنَا وَ مَوْلَانَا) مُحَمَّدٍ كَمَا صَلَّيْتَ عَلٰى اٰلِ (سَيِّدِنَا) اِبْرَاهِيْمَ وَ بَارِكْ عَلٰى (سَيِّدِنَا وَ مَوْلَانَا) مُحَمَّدٍ وَّ عَلٰى اٰلِ (سَيِّدِنَا وَ مَوْلَانَا) مُحَمَّدٍ كَمَا بَارَكْتَ عَلٰى اٰلِ (سَيِّدِنَا) اِبْرَاهِيْمَ فِي الْعَالَمِيْنَ اِنَّكَ حَمِيدٌ مَّجِيدٌ.

۱۲ اَللّٰهُمَّ صَلِّ عَلٰى (سَيِّدِنَا وَ مَوْلَانَا) مُحَمَّدٍ وَّ أَزْوَاجِهٖ وَذُرِّيَّتِهٖ كَمَاصَلَّيْتَ عَلٰى اٰلِ (سَيِّدِنَا) اِبْرَاهِيْمَ وَ بَارِكْ عَلٰى (سَيِّدِنَا وَ مَوْلَانَا) مُحَمَّدٍ وَّ اَزْوَاجِهٖ وَذُرِّيَّتِهٖ كَمَا بَارَكْتَ عَلٰى اٰلِ (سَيِّدِنَا) اِبْرَاهِيْمَ اِنَّكَ حَمِيْدٌ مَّجِيْدٌ.

۱۳ اَللّٰهُمَّ صَلِّ عَلٰى (سَيِّدِنَا وَ مَوْلَانَا) مُحَمَّدٍ وَّ عَلٰى اَزْوَاجِهٖ وَذُرِّيَّتِهٖ كَمَا صَلَّيْتَ عَلٰى اٰلِ (سَيِّدِنَا) اِبْرَاهِيْمَ وَ بَارِكْ عَلٰى (سَيِّدِنَا وَ مَوْلَانَا) مُحَمَّدٍ وَّ عَلٰى اَزْوَاجِهٖ وَذُرِّيَّتِهٖ كَمَا بَارَكْتَ عَلٰى اٰلِ (سَيِّدِنَا) اِبْرَاهِيْمَ اِنَّكَ حَمِيْدٌ مَّجِيْدٌ.

۱۴ اَللّٰهُمَّ صَلِّ عَلٰى (سَيِّدِنَا وَ مَوْلَانَا) مُحَمَّدٍ النَّبِيِّ وَ أَزْوَاجِهٖ أُمَّهَاتِ الْمُؤْمِنِيْنَ وَ ذُرِّيَّتِهٖ وَ اَهْلِ بَيْتِهٖ كَمَا صَلَّيْتَ عَلٰى (سَيِّدِنَا) اِبْرَاهِيْمَ اِنَّكَ حَمِيْدٌ مَّجِيْدٌ.

۱۵ اَللّٰهُمَّ صَلِّ عَلٰى (سَيِّدِنَا وَ مَوْلَانَا) مُحَمَّدٍ وَّ عَلٰى اٰلِ (سَيِّدِنَا وَ مَوْلَانَا) مُحَمَّدٍ كَمَا صَلَّيْتَ عَلٰى (سَيِّدِنَا) اِبْرَاهِيْمَ وَ عَلٰى اٰلِ (سَيِّدِنَا) اِبْرَاهِيْمَ وَ بَارِكْ عَلٰى (سَيِّدِنَا وَ مَوْلَانَا) مُحَمَّدٍ وَّ عَلٰى اٰلِ (سَيِّدِنَا وَ مَوْلَانَا) مُحَمَّدٍ كَمَا بَارَكْتَ عَلٰى (سَيِّدِنَا) اِبْرَاهِيْمَ ، وَ تَرَحَّمْ عَلٰى (سَيِّدِنَا وَ مَوْلَانَا) مُحَمَّدٍ وَّ عَلٰى

اٰلِ (سَيِّدِنَا وَ مَوْلَانَا) مُحَمَّدٍ كَمَا تَرَحَّمْتَ عَلٰى (سَيِّدِنَا) اِبْرَاهِيْمَ وَ عَلٰى اٰلِ (سَيِّدِنَا) اِبْرَاهِيْمَ.

۱۶ اَللّٰهُمَّ صَلِّ عَلٰى (سَيِّدِنَا وَ مَوْلَانَا) مُحَمَّدٍ وَّ عَلٰى اٰلِ (سَيِّدِنَا وَ مَوْلَانَا) مُحَمَّدٍ كَمَا صَلَّيْتَ عَلٰى (سَيِّدِنَا) اِبْرَاهِيْمَ وَ عَلٰى اٰلِ (سَيِّدِنَا) اِبْرَاهِيْمَ اِنَّكَ حَمِيْدٌ مَّجِيْدٌ ، اَللّٰهُمَّ بَارِكْ عَلٰى (سَيِّدِنَا وَ مَوْلَانَا) مُحَمَّدٍ وَّ عَلٰى اٰلِ (سَيِّدِنَا وَ مَوْلَانَا) مُحَمَّدٍ كَمَا بَارَكْتَ عَلٰى (سَيِّدِنَا) اِبْرَاهِيْمَ وَ عَلٰى اٰلِ (سَيِّدِنَا) اِبْرَاهِيْمَ اِنَّكَ حَمِيْدٌ مَّجِيْدٌ ، اَللّٰهُمَّ تَرَحَّمْ عَلٰى (سَيِّدِنَا وَ مَوْلَانَا) مُحَمَّدٍ وَّ عَلٰى اٰلِ (سَيِّدِنَا وَ مَوْلَانَا) مُحَمَّدٍ كَمَا تَرَحَّمْتَ عَلٰى (سَيِّدِنَا) اِبْرَاهِيْمَ وَ عَلٰى اٰلِ (سَيِّدِنَا) اِبْرَاهِيْمَ اِنَّكَ حَمِيْدٌ مَّجِيْدٌ ، اَللّٰهُمَّ تَحَنَّنْ عَلٰى (سَيِّدِنَا وَ مَوْلَانَا) مُحَمَّدٍ وَّ عَلٰى اٰلِ (سَيِّدِنَا وَ مَوْلَانَا) مُحَمَّدٍ كَمَا تَحَنَّنْتَ عَلٰى (سَيِّدِنَا) اِبْرَاهِيْمَ وَ عَلٰى اٰلِ (سَيِّدِنَا) اِبْرَاهِيْمَ اِنَّكَ حَمِيْدٌ مَّجِيْدٌ ، اَللّٰهُمَّ سَلِّمْ عَلٰى (سَيِّدِنَا وَ مَوْلَانَا) مُحَمَّدٍ وَّ عَلٰى اٰلِ (سَيِّدِنَا وَ مَوْلَانَا) مُحَمَّدٍ كَمَا سَلَّمْتَ عَلٰى (سَيِّدِنَا) اِبْرَاهِيْمَ وَ عَلٰى اٰلِ (سَيِّدِنَا) اِبْرَاهِيْمَ اِنَّكَ حَمِيْدٌ مَّجِيْدٌ.

۱۷ اَللّٰهُمَّ صَلِّ عَلٰى (سَيِّدِنَا وَ مَوْلَانَا) مُحَمَّدٍ وَّ عَلٰى اٰلِ (سَيِّدِنَا وَ مَوْلَانَا)

مُحَمَّدٍ وَّ بَارِكْ وَ سَلِّمْ عَلٰى (سَيِّدِنَا وَ مَوْلَانَا) مُحَمَّدٍ وَّ عَلٰى اٰلِ (سَيِّدِنَا وَ

مَوْلَانَا) مُحَمَّدٍ وَّ ارْحَمْ (سَيِّدَنَا وَ مَوْلَانَا) مُحَمَّدًا وَّ اٰلَ (سَيِّدِنَا وَ مَوْلَانَا)

مُحَمَّدٍ كَمَا صَلَّيْتَ وَ بَارَكْتَ وَ تَرَحَّمْتَ عَلٰى (سَيِّدِنَا) اِبْرَاهِيْمَ وَ عَلٰى اٰلِ

(سَيِّدِنَا) اِبْرَاهِيْمَ فِي الْعَالَمِيْنَ اِنَّكَ حَمِيْدٌ مَّجِيْدٌ.

۱۸ ۝ اَللّٰهُمَّ صَلِّ عَلٰى (سَيِّدِنَا وَ مَوْلَانَا) مُحَمَّدٍ وَّ عَلٰى اٰلِ (سَيِّدِنَا وَ مَوْلَانَا)

مُحَمَّدٍ كَمَا صَلَّيْتَ عَلٰى (سَيِّدِنَا) اِبْرَاهِيْمَ وَ عَلٰى اٰلِ (سَيِّدِنَا) اِبْرَاهِيْمَ اِنَّكَ

حَمِيْدٌ مَّجِيْدٌ ، اَللّٰهُمَّ بَارِكْ عَلٰى (سَيِّدِنَا وَ مَوْلَانَا) مُحَمَّدٍ وَّ عَلٰى اٰلِ (سَيِّدِنَا وَ

مَوْلَانَا) مُحَمَّدٍ كَمَا بَارَكْتَ عَلٰى (سَيِّدِنَا) اِبْرَاهِيْمَ وَ عَلٰى اٰلِ (سَيِّدِنَا)

اِبْرَاهِيْمَ اِنَّكَ حَمِيْدٌ مَّجِيْدٌ.

۱۹ ۝ اَللّٰهُمَّ صَلِّ عَلٰى (سَيِّدِنَا وَ مَوْلَانَا) مُحَمَّدٍ عَبْدِكَ وَ رَسُوْلِكَ كَمَا صَلَّيْتَ

عَلٰى اٰلِ اِبْرَاهِيْمَ وَ بَارِكْ عَلٰى (سَيِّدِنَا وَ مَوْلَانَا) مُحَمَّدٍ وَّ عَلٰى اٰلِ (سَيِّدِنَا وَ

مَوْلَانَا) مُحَمَّدٍ كَمَا بَارَكْتَ عَلٰى اٰلِ (سَيِّدِنَا) اِبْرَاهِيْمَ.

۲۰ ۝ اَللّٰهُمَّ صَلِّ عَلٰى (سَيِّدِنَا وَ مَوْلَانَا) مُحَمَّدٍ النَّبِيِّ الْأُمِّيِّ وَ عَلٰى اٰلِ (سَيِّدِنَا وَ

مَوْلَانَا) مُحَمَّدٍ كَمَا صَلَّيْتَ عَلٰى (سَيِّدِنَا) اِبْرَاهِيْمَ وَ بَارِكْ عَلٰى (سَيِّدِنَا وَ

مَوْلَانَا) مُحَمَّدٍ النَّبِيِّ الْأُمِّيِّ كَمَا بَارَكْتَ عَلَى (سَيِّدِنَا) اِبْرَاهِيمَ اِنَّكَ حَمِيدٌ مَّجِيدٌ.

㉑ اَللّٰهُمَّ صَلِّ عَلَى (سَيِّدِنَا وَ مَوْلَانَا) مُحَمَّدٍ عَبْدِكَ وَ رَسُوْلِكَ النَّبِيِّ الْأُمِّيِّ وَ عَلَى اٰلِ (سَيِّدِنَا وَ مَوْلَانَا) مُحَمَّدٍ ، أَللّٰهُمَّ صَلِّ عَلَى (سَيِّدِنَا وَ مَوْلَانَا) مُحَمَّدٍ وَّ عَلَى اٰلِ (سَيِّدِنَا وَ مَوْلَانَا) مُحَمَّدٍ صَلٰوةً تَكُوْنُ لَكَ رِضًى وَّ لَهٗ جَزَاءً وَّ لِحَقِّهِ أَدَاءً ، وَّ اَعْطِهِ الْوَسِيْلَةَ وَ الْفَضِيْلَةَ وَ الْمَقَامَ الْمَحْمُوْدَ الَّذِيْ وَعَدْتَّهٗ وَ اجْزِهٖ عَنَّا مَا هُوَ أَهْلُهٗ؍وَ اجْزِهٖ أَفْضَلَ مَا جَازَيْتَ نَبِيًّا عَنْ قَوْمِهٖ وَ رَسُوْلًا عَنْ أُمَّتِهٖ ، وَ صَلِّ عَلَى جَمِيْعِ اِخْوَانِهٖ مِنَ النَّبِيِّيْنَ وَ الصَّالِحِيْنَ يَا اَرْحَمَ الرَّاحِمِيْنَ.

㉒ اَللّٰهُمَّ صَلِّ عَلَى (سَيِّدِنَا وَ مَوْلَانَا) مُحَمَّدٍ النَّبِيِّ الْأُمِّيِّ وَ عَلَى اٰلِ (سَيِّدِنَا وَ مَوْلَانَا) مُحَمَّدٍ كَمَا صَلَّيْتَ عَلَى (سَيِّدِنَا) اِبْرَاهِيْمَ وَ عَلَى اٰلِ (سَيِّدِنَا) اِبْرَاهِيْمَ ، وَ بَارِكْ عَلَى (سَيِّدِنَا وَ مَوْلَانَا) مُحَمَّدٍ النَّبِيِّ الْأُمِّيِّ وَ عَلَى اٰلِ (سَيِّدِنَا وَ مَوْلَانَا) مُحَمَّدٍ كَمَا بَارَكْتَ عَلَى (سَيِّدِنَا) اِبْرَاهِيْمَ وَ عَلَى اٰلِ

(سَيِّدِنَا) اِبْرَاهِيْمَ اِنَّكَ حَمِيْدٌ مَجِيْدٌ.

۲۳ اَللّٰهُمَّ صَلِّ عَلَى (سَيِّدِنَا وَ مَوْلَانَا) مُحَمَّدٍ وَّ عَلَى اٰهِلِ بَيْتِهٖ كَمَا صَلَّيْتَ عَلَى (سَيِّدِنَا) اِبْرَاهِيْمَ اِنَّكَ حَمِيْدٌ مَجِيْدٌ ، اَللّٰهُمَّ صَلِّ عَلَيْنَا مَعَهُمْ ، اَللّٰهُمَّ بَارِكْ عَلَى (سَيِّدِنَا وَ مَوْلَانَا) مُحَمَّدٍ وَّ عَلَى أَهْلِ بَيْتِهٖ كَمَا بَارَكْتَ عَلَى (سَيِّدِنَا) اِبْرَاهِيْمَ اِنَّكَ حَمِيْدٌ مَجِيْدٌ ، اَللّٰهُمَّ بَارِكْ عَلَيْنَا مَعَهُمْ ، صَلَوَاتُ اللهِ وَ صَلَوَاتُ الْمُؤْمِنِيْنَ عَلَى مُحَمَّدٍ النَّبِيِّ الْأُمِّيِّ.

۲٤ اَللّٰهُمَّ اجْعَلْ صَلَوَاتِكَ وَ رَحْمَتَكَ وَ بَرَكَاتِكَ عَلَى (سَيِّدِنَا وَ مَوْلَانَا) مُحَمَّدٍ وَّ عَلَى اٰلِ (سَيِّدِنَا وَ مَوْلَانَا) مُحَمَّدٍ كَمَا جَعَلْتَهَا عَلَى (سَيِّدِنَا) اِبْرَاهِيْمَ وَ عَلَى اٰلِ (سَيِّدِنَا) اِبْرَاهِيْمَ اِنَّكَ حَمِيْدٌ مَجِيْدٌ وَ بَارِكْ عَلَى (سَيِّدِنَا وَ مَوْلَانَا) مُحَمَّدٍ وَّ عَلَى اٰلِ (سَيِّدِنَا وَ مَوْلَانَا) مُحَمَّدٍ كَمَا بَارَكْتَ عَلَى (سَيِّدِنَا) اِبْرَاهِيْمَ وَ عَلَى اٰلِ (سَيِّدِنَا) اِبْرَاهِيْمَ اِنَّكَ حَمِيْدٌ مَجِيْدٌ.

۲٥ وَ صَلَّى اللهُ عَلَى النَّبِيِّ الْأُمِّيِّ.

۲٦ اَلتَّحِيَّاتُ لِلّٰهِ وَ الصَّلَوَاتُ وَ الطَّيِّبَاتُ ، اَلسَّلَامُ عَلَيْكَ أَيُّهَا النَّبِيُّ وَ رَحْمَةُ اللهِ وَ بَرَكَاتُهُ، اَلسَّلَامُ عَلَيْنَا وَ عَلَى عِبَادِ اللهِ الصَّالِحِيْنَ، أَشْهَدُ أَنْ

لَّا اِلٰهَ اِلَّا اللهُ وَ اَشْهَدُ أَنَّ (سَيِّدَنَا وَ مَوْلَانَا) مُحَمَّدًا عَبْدُهُ وَ رَسُولُهُ.

۲۷ اَلتَّحِيَّاتُ الطَّيِّبَاتُ الصَّلَوَاتُ لِلهِ ، اَلسَّلَامُ عَلَيْكَ اَيُّهَا النَّبِيُّ وَ رَحْمَةُ اللهِ وَ بَرَكَاتُهُ، اَلسَّلَامُ عَلَيْنَا وَ عَلٰى عِبَادِ اللهِ الصَّالِحِينَ ، أَشْهَدُ أَنْ لَّا اِلٰهَ اِلَّا اللهُ وَ أَشْهَدُ أَنَّ (سَيِّدَنَا وَ مَوْلَانَا) مُحَمَّدًا عَبْدُهُ وَ رَسُولُهُ.

۲۸ اَلتَّحِيَّاتُ لِلهِ الطَّيِّبَاتُ الصَّلَوَاتُ لِلهِ ، اَلسَّلَامُ عَلَيْكَ اَيُّهَا النَّبِيُّ وَ رَحْمَةُ اللهِ وَ بَرَكَاتُهُ، اَلسَّلَامُ عَلَيْنَا وَ عَلٰى عِبَادِ اللهِ الصَّالِحِينَ ، أَشْهَدُ أَنْ لَّا اِلٰهَ اِلَّا اللهُ وَحْدَهُ لَا شَرِيكَ لَهُ وَ اَشْهَدُ اَنَّ (سَيِّدَنَا وَ مَوْلَانَا) مُحَمَّدًا عَبْدُهُ وَ رَسُولُهُ.

۲۹ اَلتَّحِيَّاتُ الْمُبَارَكَاتُ الصَّلَوَاتُ الطَّيِّبَاتُ لِلهِ ، سَلَامٌ عَلَيْكَ اَيُّهَا النَّبِيُّ وَ رَحْمَةُ اللهِ وَ بَرَكَاتُهُ، سَلَامٌ عَلَيْنَا وَ عَلٰى عِبَادِ اللهِ الصَّالِحِينَ ، اَشْهَدُ أَنْ لَّا اِلٰهَ اِلَّا اللهُ وَ اَشْهَدُ اَنَّ (سَيِّدَنَا وَ مَوْلَانَا) مُحَمَّدًا عَبْدُهُ وَ رَسُولُهُ.

۳۰ بِسْمِ اللهِ وَ بِاللهِ ، اَلتَّحِيَّاتُ لِلهِ وَ الصَّلَوَاتُ وَ الطَّيِّبَاتُ ، اَلسَّلَامُ عَلَيْكَ اَيُّهَا النَّبِيُّ وَ رَحْمَةُ اللهِ وَ بَرَكَاتُهُ، اَلسَّلَامُ عَلَيْنَا وَ عَلٰى عِبَادِ اللهِ الصَّالِحِينَ ، اَشْهَدُ انْ لَّا اِلٰهَ اِلَّا اللهُ وَ اَشْهَدُ اَنَّ (سَيِّدَنَا وَ مَوْلَانَا) مُحَمَّدًا

عَبْدُهُ وَ رَسُوْلُهُ، اَسْأَلُ اللهَ الْجَنَّةَ وَ اَعُوْذُ بِاللهِ مِنَ النَّارِ.

(۳۱) اَلتَّحِيَّاتُ لِلّٰهِ الزَّاكِيَاتُ لِلّٰهِ الطَّيِّبَاتُ الصَّلَوَاتُ لِلّٰهِ ، اَلسَّلَامُ عَلَيْكَ اَيُّهَا النَّبِيُّ وَ رَحْمَةُ اللهِ وَ بَرَكَاتُهُ ، اَلسَّلَامُ عَلَيْنَا وَ عَلٰى عِبَادِ اللهِ الصَّالِحِيْنَ ، اَشْهَدُ أَنْ لَّا اِلٰهَ اِلَّا اللهُ وَ اَشْهَدُ اَنَّ (سَيِّدَنَا وَ مَوْلَانَا) مُحَمَّدًا عَبْدُهُ وَ رَسُوْلُهُ.

(۳۲) بِسْمِ اللهِ وَ بِاللهِ خَيْرِ الْأَسْمَاءِ ، اَلتَّحِيَّاتُ الطَّيِّبَاتُ الصَّلَوَاتُ لِلّٰهِ ، اَشْهَدُ أَنْ لَّا اِلٰهَ اِلَّا اللهُ وَحْدَهُ، لَا شَرِيْكَ لَهُ، وَ اَشْهَدُ اَنَّ (سَيِّدَنَا وَ مَوْلَانَا) مُحَمَّدًا عَبْدُهُ وَ رَسُوْلُهُ، اَرْسَلَهُ بِالْحَقِّ بَشِيْرًا وَّ نَذِيْرًا ، وَاَنَّ السَّاعَةَ اٰتِيَةٌ لَّا رَيْبَ فِيْهَا ، اَلسَّلَامُ عَلَيْكَ اَيُّهَا النَّبِيُّ وَ رَحْمَةُ اللهِ وَ بَرَكَاتُهُ، اَلسَّلَامُ عَلَيْنَا وَ عَلٰى عِبَادِ اللهِ الصَّالِحِيْنَ اَللّٰهُمَّ اغْفِرْلِيْ وَاهْدِنِيْ.

(۳۳) اَلتَّحِيَّاتُ الطَّيِّبَاتُ وَ الصَّلَوَاتُ وَ الْمُلْكُ لِلّٰهِ ، اَلسَّلَامُ عَلَيْكَ اَيُّهَا النَّبِيُّ وَ رَحْمَةُ اللهِ وَ بَرَكَاتُهُ:

(۳٤) بِسْمِ اللهِ ، اَلتَّحِيَّاتُ لِلّٰهِ الصَّلَوَاتُ لِلّٰهِ الزَّاكِيَاتُ لِلّٰهِ ، اَلسَّلَامُ عَلَى النَّبِيِّ وَ رَحْمَةُ اللهِ وَ بَرَكَاتُهُ، اَلسَّلَامُ عَلَيْنَا وَ عَلٰى عِبَادِ اللهِ الصَّالِحِيْنَ ، شَهِدْتُ

أَنْ لَا إِلٰهَ إِلَّا اللهُ شَهِدْتُ أَنَّ (سَيِّدَنَا وَ مَوْلَانَا) مُحَمَّدًا رَسُوْلُ اللهِ.

(٣٥) اَلتَّحِيَّاتُ الطَّيِّبَاتُ الصَّلَوَاتُ الزَّاكِيَاتُ لِلهِ، اَشْهَدُ أَنْ لَّا اِلٰهَ إِلَّا اللهُ وَحْدَهُ لَا شَرِيكَ لَهُ وَ اَنَّ (سَيِّدَنَا وَ مَوْلَانَا) مُحَمَّدًا عَبْدُهُ وَ رَسُوْلُهُ، اَلسَّلَامُ عَلَيْكَ اَيُّهَا النَّبِيُّ وَ رَحْمَةُ اللهِ وَ بَرَكَاتُهُ، اَلسَّلَامُ عَلَيْنَا وَ عَلٰى عِبَادِ اللهِ الصَّالِحِيْنَ.

(٣٦) اَلتَّحِيَّاتُ الطَّيِّبَاتُ الصَّلَوَاتُ الزَّاكِيَاتُ لِلهِ، اَشْهَدُ أَنْ لَّا اِلٰهَ اِلَّا اللهُ وَ اَشْهَدُ اَنَّ (سَيِّدَنَا وَ مَوْلَانَا) مُحَمَّدًا عَبْدُ اللهِ وَ رَسُوْلُهُ، اَلسَّلَامُ عَلَيْكَ اَيُّهَا النَّبِيُّ وَ رَحْمَةُ اللهِ وَ بَرَكَاتُهُ، اَلسَّلَامُ عَلَيْنَا وَ عَلٰى عِبَادِ اللهِ الصَّالِحِيْنَ.

(٣٧) اَلتَّحِيَّاتُ الصَّلَوَاتُ لِلهِ، اَلسَّلَامُ عَلَيْكَ اَيُّهَا النَّبِيُّ وَ رَحْمَةُ اللهِ وَ بَرَكَاتُهُ، اَلسَّلَامُ عَلَيْنَا وَ عَلٰى عِبَادِ اللهِ الصَّالِحِيْنَ.

(٣٨) اَلتَّحِيَّاتُ لِلهِ الصَّلَوَاتُ الطَّيِّبَاتُ، اَلسَّلَامُ عَلَيْكَ اَيُّهَا النَّبِيُّ وَ رَحْمَةُ اللهِ اَلسَّلَامُ عَلَيْنَا وَ عَلٰى عِبَادِ اللهِ الصَّالِحِيْنَ اَشْهَدُ اَنْ لَّا اِلٰهَ اِلَّا اللهُ وَ اَشْهَدُ اَنَّ (سَيِّدَنَا وَ مَوْلَانَا) مُحَمَّدًا عَبْدُهُ وَ رَسُوْلُهُ،

(٣٩) اَلتَّحِيَّاتُ الْمُبَارَكَاتُ الصَّلَوَاتُ الطَّيِّبَاتُ لِلهِ، اَلسَّلَامُ عَلَيْكَ اَيُّهَا النَّبِيُّ

وَ رَحْمَةُ اللهِ وَ بَرَكَاتُهُ ، اَلسَّلَامُ عَلَيْنَا وَ عَلَى عِبَادِ اللهِ الصَّالِحِيْنَ ، اَشْهَدُ اَنْ

لَّا اِلٰهَ اِلَّا اللهُ وَ اَشْهَدُ اَنَّ (سَيِّدَنَا وَ مَوْلَانَا) مُحَمَّدًا رَّسُوْلُ اللهِ.

بِسْمِ اللهِ وَ السَّلَامُ عَلَى رَسُوْلِ اللهِ.

# MANZIL

بِسْمِ اللهِ الرَّحْمٰنِ الرَّحِيْمِ

اَلْحَمْدُ لِلّٰهِ رَبِّ الْعٰلَمِيْنَ ۞ اَلرَّحْمٰنِ الرَّحِيْمِ ۞ مٰلِكِ يَوْمِ الدِّيْنِ ۞ اِيَّاكَ نَعْبُدُ وَاِيَّاكَ نَسْتَعِيْنُ ۞ اِهْدِنَا الصِّرٰطَ الْمُسْتَقِيْمَ ۞ صِرٰطَ الَّذِيْنَ اَنْعَمْتَ عَلَيْهِمْ ۞ غَيْرِ الْمَغْضُوْبِ عَلَيْهِمْ وَلَا الضَّآلِّيْنَ ۞

بِسْمِ اللهِ الرَّحْمٰنِ الرَّحِيْمِ

الٓمّٓ ۞ ذٰلِكَ الْكِتٰبُ لَا رَيْبَ فِيْهِ هُدًى لِّلْمُتَّقِيْنَ ۞ الَّذِيْنَ يُؤْمِنُوْنَ بِالْغَيْبِ وَيُقِيْمُوْنَ الصَّلٰوةَ وَمِمَّا رَزَقْنٰهُمْ يُنْفِقُوْنَ ۞ وَالَّذِيْنَ يُؤْمِنُوْنَ بِمَآ اُنْزِلَ اِلَيْكَ وَمَآ اُنْزِلَ مِنْ قَبْلِكَ وَبِالْاٰخِرَةِ هُمْ يُوْقِنُوْنَ ۞ اُولٰٓئِكَ عَلٰى هُدًى مِّنْ رَّبِّهِمْ وَاُولٰٓئِكَ هُمُ الْمُفْلِحُوْنَ ۞

وَاِلٰهُكُمْ اِلٰهٌ وَّاحِدٌ لَّا اِلٰهَ اِلَّا هُوَ الرَّحْمٰنُ الرَّحِيْمُ ۝١٦٣

اَللّٰهُ لَآ اِلٰهَ اِلَّا هُوَ الْحَىُّ الْقَيُّوْمُ ۚ لَا تَأْخُذُهٗ سِنَةٌ وَّلَا نَوْمٌ ۚ لَهٗ مَا فِى السَّمٰوٰتِ وَمَا فِى الْاَرْضِ ۗ مَنْ ذَا الَّذِىْ يَشْفَعُ عِنْدَهٗٓ اِلَّا بِاِذْنِهٖ ۚ يَعْلَمُ مَا بَيْنَ اَيْدِيْهِمْ وَمَا خَلْفَهُمْ ۖ وَلَا يُحِيْطُوْنَ بِشَىْءٍ مِّنْ عِلْمِهٖٓ اِلَّا بِمَا شَآءَ ۚ وَسِعَ كُرْسِيُّهُ السَّمٰوٰتِ وَالْاَرْضَ ۚ وَلَا يَئُوْدُهٗ حِفْظُهُمَا ۚ وَهُوَ الْعَلِىُّ الْعَظِيْمُ ۝ لَآ إِكْرَاهَ فِى الدِّيْنِ ۚ قَدْ تَّبَيَّنَ الرُّشْدُ مِنَ الْغَىِّ ۚ فَمَنْ يَّكْفُرْ بِالطَّاغُوْتِ وَيُؤْمِنْ بِاللّٰهِ فَقَدِ اسْتَمْسَكَ بِالْعُرْوَةِ الْوُثْقٰى لَا انْفِصَامَ لَهَا ۗ وَاللّٰهُ سَمِيْعٌ عَلِيْمٌ ۝ اَللّٰهُ وَلِىُّ الَّذِيْنَ اٰمَنُوْا يُخْرِجُهُمْ مِّنَ الظُّلُمٰتِ إِلَى النُّوْرِ ۚ وَالَّذِيْنَ كَفَرُوْٓا اَوْلِيَآؤُهُمُ الطَّاغُوْتُ يُخْرِجُوْنَهُمْ مِّنَ النُّوْرِ إِلَى الظُّلُمٰتِ ۚ أُولٰٓئِكَ أَصْحٰبُ النَّارِ ۖ هُمْ فِيْهَا خٰلِدُوْنَ ۝

لِلّٰهِ مَا فِى السَّمٰوٰتِ وَمَا فِى الْاَرْضِ ۗ وَإِنْ تُبْدُوْا مَا فِىْٓ أَنْفُسِكُمْ أَوْ تُخْفُوْهُ يُحَاسِبْكُمْ بِهِ اللّٰهُ ۖ فَيَغْفِرُ لِمَنْ يَّشَآءُ وَيُعَذِّبُ مَنْ يَّشَآءُ ۗ وَاللّٰهُ عَلٰى كُلِّ شَىْءٍ قَدِيْرٌ ۝ اٰمَنَ الرَّسُوْلُ بِمَآ أُنْزِلَ اِلَيْهِ مِنْ رَّبِّهٖ وَالْمُؤْمِنُوْنَ ۚ كُلٌّ اٰمَنَ بِاللّٰهِ وَمَلٰٓئِكَتِهٖ وَكُتُبِهٖ وَرُسُلِهٖ لَا نُفَرِّقُ بَيْنَ أَحَدٍ مِّنْ رُّسُلِهٖ ۚ وَقَالُوْا سَمِعْنَا وَأَطَعْنَا غُفْرَانَكَ رَبَّنَا

وَاِلَيْكَ الْمَصِيرُ ۝ لَا يُكَلِّفُ اللهُ نَفْسًا اِلَّا وُسْعَهَا ۚ لَهَا مَا

كَسَبَتْ وَعَلَيْهَا مَا اكْتَسَبَتْ ۗ رَبَّنَا لَا تُؤَاخِذْنَآ اِنْ نَّسِينَآ أَوْ

أَخْطَأْنَا ۚ رَبَّنَا وَلَا تَحْمِلْ عَلَيْنَآ اِصْرًا كَمَا حَمَلْتَهُ عَلَى الَّذِينَ مِنْ

قَبْلِنَا ۚ رَبَّنَا وَلَا تُحَمِّلْنَا مَا لَا طَاقَةَ لَنَا بِهِ ۖ وَاعْفُ عَنَّا وَاغْفِرْ

لَنَا وَارْحَمْنَا ۚ أَنْتَ مَوْلَىٰنَا فَانْصُرْنَا عَلَى الْقَوْمِ الْكَافِرِينَ ۝

شَهِدَ اللهُ أَنَّهُ لَآ اِلٰهَ اِلَّا هُوَ وَالْمَلٰٓئِكَةُ وَأُولُوا الْعِلْمِ قَآئِمًا

بِالْقِسْطِ ۚ لَآ اِلٰهَ اِلَّا هُوَ الْعَزِيزُ الْحَكِيمُ ۝

قُلِ اللّٰهُمَّ مٰلِكَ الْمُلْكِ تُؤْتِى الْمُلْكَ مَنْ تَشَآءُ وَتَنْزِعُ الْمُلْكَ

مِمَّنْ تَشَآءُ وَتُعِزُّ مَنْ تَشَآءُ وَتُذِلُّ مَنْ تَشَآءُ ۖ بِيَدِكَ الْخَيْرُ ۗ اِنَّكَ

عَلَىٰ كُلِّ شَىْءٍ قَدِيرٌ ۝ تُولِجُ الَّيْلَ فِى النَّهَارِ وَتُولِجُ النَّهَارَ فِى

الَّيْلِ ۖ وَتُخْرِجُ الْحَىَّ مِنَ الْمَيِّتِ وَتُخْرِجُ الْمَيِّتَ مِنَ الْحَىِّ

وَتَرْزُقُ مَنْ تَشَآءُ بِغَيْرِ حِسَابٍ ۝

اِنَّ رَبَّكُمُ اللّٰهُ الَّذِىْ خَلَقَ السَّمٰوٰتِ وَالْاَرْضَ فِىْ سِتَّةِ اَيَّامٍ ثُمَّ اسْتَوٰى عَلَى الْعَرْشِ يُغْشِى الَّيْلَ النَّهَارَ يَطْلُبُهٗ حَثِيْثًا وَّالشَّمْسَ وَالْقَمَرَ وَالنُّجُوْمَ مُسَخَّرٰتٍۭ بِاَمْرِهٖ اَلَا لَهُ الْخَلْقُ وَالْاَمْرُ تَبَارَكَ اللّٰهُ رَبُّ الْعٰلَمِيْنَ ۵۴ اُدْعُوْا رَبَّكُمْ تَضَرُّعًا وَّخُفْيَةً اِنَّهٗ لَا يُحِبُّ الْمُعْتَدِيْنَ ۵۵ وَلَا تُفْسِدُوْا فِى الْاَرْضِ بَعْدَ اِصْلَاحِهَا وَادْعُوْهُ خَوْفًا وَّطَمَعًا اِنَّ رَحْمَتَ اللّٰهِ قَرِيْبٌ مِّنَ الْمُحْسِنِيْنَ ۵۶

قُلِ ادْعُوا اللّٰهَ اَوِ ادْعُوا الرَّحْمٰنَ اَيًّا مَّا تَدْعُوْا فَلَهُ الْاَسْمَآءُ الْحُسْنٰى وَلَا تَجْهَرْ بِصَلَاتِكَ وَلَا تُخَافِتْ بِهَا وَابْتَغِ بَيْنَ ذٰلِكَ سَبِيْلًا ۱۱۰ وَقُلِ الْحَمْدُ لِلّٰهِ الَّذِىْ لَمْ يَتَّخِذْ وَلَدًا وَّلَمْ يَكُنْ لَّهٗ شَرِيْكٌ فِى الْمُلْكِ وَلَمْ يَكُنْ لَّهٗ وَلِيٌّ مِّنَ الذُّلِّ وَكَبِّرْهُ تَكْبِيْرًا ۱۱۱

اَفَحَسِبْتُمْ اَنَّمَا خَلَقْنٰكُمْ عَبَثًا وَّاَنَّكُمْ اِلَيْنَا لَا تُرْجَعُوْنَ ۱۱۵ فَتَعٰلَى اللّٰهُ الْمَلِكُ الْحَقُّ لَاۤ اِلٰهَ اِلَّا هُوَ رَبُّ الْعَرْشِ الْكَرِيْمِ ۱۱۶ وَمَنْ يَّدْعُ مَعَ اللّٰهِ اِلٰهًا اٰخَرَ لَا بُرْهَانَ لَهٗ بِهٖ فَاِنَّمَا حِسَابُهٗ عِنْدَ

رَبِّهِ ۗ اِنَّهُ لَا يُفْلِحُ الْكَافِرُوْنَ ۝ وَقُلْ رَّبِّ اغْفِرْ وَارْحَمْ وَاَنْتَ خَيْرُ الرَّاحِمِيْنَ ۝

بِسْمِ اللّٰهِ الرَّحْمٰنِ الرَّحِيْمِ

وَالصّٰٓفّٰتِ صَفًّا ۝ فَالزّٰجِرٰتِ زَجْرًا ۝ فَالتّٰلِيٰتِ ذِكْرًا ۝ اِنَّ اِلٰهَكُمْ لَوَاحِدٌ ۝ رَبُّ السَّمٰوٰتِ وَالْاَرْضِ وَمَا بَيْنَهُمَا وَرَبُّ الْمَشَارِقِ ۝ اِنَّا زَيَّنَّا السَّمَآءَ الدُّنْيَا بِزِيْنَةِ الْكَوَاكِبِ ۝ وَحِفْظًا مِّنْ كُلِّ شَيْطٰنٍ مَّارِدٍ ۝ لَا يَسَّمَّعُوْنَ اِلَى الْمَلَاِ الْاَعْلٰى وَيُقْذَفُوْنَ مِنْ كُلِّ جَانِبٍ ۝ دُحُوْرًا وَّلَهُمْ عَذَابٌ وَّاصِبٌ ۝ اِلَّا مَنْ خَطِفَ الْخَطْفَةَ فَاَتْبَعَهُ شِهَابٌ ثَاقِبٌ ۝ فَاسْتَفْتِهِمْ اَهُمْ اَشَدُّ خَلْقًا اَمْ مَّنْ خَلَقْنَا ۚ اِنَّا خَلَقْنٰهُمْ مِّنْ طِيْنٍ لَّازِبٍ ۝

يٰمَعْشَرَ الْجِنِّ وَالْاِنْسِ اِنِ اسْتَطَعْتُمْ اَنْ تَنْفُذُوْا مِنْ اَقْطَارِ السَّمٰوٰتِ وَالْاَرْضِ فَانْفُذُوْا ۗ لَا تَنْفُذُوْنَ اِلَّا بِسُلْطٰنٍ ۝ فَبِاَيِّ اٰلَآءِ رَبِّكُمَا تُكَذِّبٰنِ ۝ يُرْسَلُ عَلَيْكُمَا شُوَاظٌ مِّنْ نَّارٍ وَّنُحَاسٌ فَلَا تَنْتَصِرَانِ ۝ فَبِاَيِّ اٰلَآءِ رَبِّكُمَا تُكَذِّبٰنِ ۝ فَاِذَا

انْشَقَّتِ السَّمَآءُ فَكَانَتْ وَرْدَةً كَالدِّهَانِ ۞ فَبِأَيِّ اٰلَآءِ رَبِّكُمَا تُكَذِّبَانِ ۞ فَيَوْمَئِذٍ لَّا يُسْئَلُ عَنْ ذَنْۢبِهٖٓ اِنْسٌ وَّلَا جَآنٌّ ۞ فَبِأَيِّ اٰلَآءِ رَبِّكُمَا تُكَذِّبَانِ ۞

لَوْ اَنْزَلْنَا هٰذَا الْقُرْاٰنَ عَلٰى جَبَلٍ لَّرَاَيْتَهٗ خَاشِعًا مُّتَصَدِّعًا مِّنْ خَشْيَةِ اللّٰهِ ۚ وَتِلْكَ الْاَمْثَالُ نَضْرِبُهَا لِلنَّاسِ لَعَلَّهُمْ يَتَفَكَّرُوْنَ ۞ هُوَ اللّٰهُ الَّذِىْ لَآ اِلٰهَ اِلَّا هُوَ ۚ عٰلِمُ الْغَيْبِ وَالشَّهَادَةِ ۚ هُوَ الرَّحْمٰنُ الرَّحِيْمُ ۞ هُوَ اللّٰهُ الَّذِىْ لَآ اِلٰهَ اِلَّا هُوَ ۚ اَلْمَلِكُ الْقُدُّوْسُ السَّلٰمُ الْمُؤْمِنُ الْمُهَيْمِنُ الْعَزِيْزُ الْجَبَّارُ الْمُتَكَبِّرُ ۚ سُبْحٰنَ اللّٰهِ عَمَّا يُشْرِكُوْنَ ۞ هُوَ اللّٰهُ الْخَالِقُ الْبَارِئُ الْمُصَوِّرُ لَهُ الْاَسْمَآءُ الْحُسْنٰى ۚ يُسَبِّحُ لَهٗ مَا فِى السَّمٰوٰتِ وَالْاَرْضِ ۚ وَهُوَ الْعَزِيْزُ الْحَكِيْمُ ۞

بِسْمِ اللهِ الرَّحْمٰنِ الرَّحِيْمِ

قُلْ اُوْحِيَ اِلَيَّ اَنَّهُ اسْتَمَعَ نَفَرٌ مِّنَ الْجِنِّ فَقَالُوْا اِنَّا سَمِعْنَا قُرْاٰنًا عَجَبًا ۝ يَهْدِيْ اِلَى الرُّشْدِ فَاٰمَنَّا بِهٖ ۖ وَلَنْ نُّشْرِكَ بِرَبِّنَا اَحَدًا ۝ وَّاَنَّهٗ تَعٰلٰى جَدُّ رَبِّنَا مَا اتَّخَذَ صٰحِبَةً وَّلَا وَلَدًا ۝ وَّاَنَّهٗ كَانَ يَقُوْلُ سَفِيْهُنَا عَلَى اللهِ شَطَطًا ۝

بِسْمِ اللهِ الرَّحْمٰنِ الرَّحِيْمِ

قُلْ يٰۤاَيُّهَا الْكٰفِرُوْنَ ۝ لَاۤ اَعْبُدُ مَا تَعْبُدُوْنَ ۝ وَلَاۤ اَنْتُمْ عٰبِدُوْنَ مَاۤ اَعْبُدُ ۝ وَلَاۤ اَنَا عَابِدٌ مَّا عَبَدْتُّمْ ۝ وَلَاۤ اَنْتُمْ عٰبِدُوْنَ مَاۤ اَعْبُدُ ۝ لَكُمْ دِيْنُكُمْ وَلِيَ دِيْنِ ۝

بِسْمِ اللهِ الرَّحْمٰنِ الرَّحِيْمِ

قُلْ هُوَ اللهُ اَحَدٌ ۝ اَللهُ الصَّمَدُ ۝ لَمْ يَلِدْ وَلَمْ يُوْلَدْ ۝ وَلَمْ يَكُنْ لَّهٗ كُفُوًا اَحَدٌ ۝

بِسْمِ اللهِ الرَّحْمٰنِ الرَّحِيْمِ

قُلْ اَعُوْذُ بِرَبِّ الْفَلَقِ ۞ مِنْ شَرِّ مَا خَلَقَ ۞ وَمِنْ شَرِّ غَاسِقٍ اِذَا وَقَبَ ۞ وَمِنْ شَرِّ النَّفّٰثٰتِ فِي الْعُقَدِ ۞ وَمِنْ شَرِّ حَاسِدٍ اِذَا حَسَدَ ۞

بِسْمِ اللهِ الرَّحْمٰنِ الرَّحِيْمِ

قُلْ اَعُوْذُ بِرَبِّ النَّاسِ ۞ مَلِكِ النَّاسِ ۞ إِلٰهِ النَّاسِ ۞ مِنْ شَرِّ الْوَسْوَاسِ الْخَنَّاسِ ۞ الَّذِيْ يُوَسْوِسُ فِيْ صُدُوْرِ النَّاسِ ۞ مِنَ الْجِنَّةِ وَالنَّاسِ ۞

The manzil has proven to be extremely effective for protection against evil influence of jinn and sihr (witchcraft). This manzil is amongst the tried and tested duas and formulas of Hadhrat Shaikh Muhammad Zakariyya (RA) as well other great Mashaaikh.

# ABRIDGED SALAATUT-TASBIH

The detailed procedure of Salaatut-Tasbih is written in the book of Hadhrat Shaikhul-Hadith Saahib *(rahmatullahi alayh)*, "Virtues of Zikr". It is recommended in the daily ma'moolaat of Hadhrat Shaikh *(rahmatullahi alayh)* that this salaah should be performed every Friday. In this particular version of Salaatut-Tasbih, the third Kalimah is recited three-hundred times. But there is another version of Salaatut-Tasbih also mentioned in a Hadith, which has, by experience, proven to be effective for the fulfillment of all worldly and spiritual objectives. The Mashaa-ikh have called it as 'Salaatut-Tasbih-As-Sughra' (the small Salaatut-Tasbih)."

The procedure for this salaah is as follows: A Hadith, reported from Hadhrat Anas-bin-Maalik رَضِىَ اللهُ عَنْهُ is mentioned by Imam Ahmad رَحِمَهُ اللهُ in his "Musnad" and also by Imaam Tirmizi رَحِمَهُ اللهُ in the "section of Salaatut Tasbih" by Imaam Nasaai رَحِمَهُ اللهُ in his "Sunan", by Ibne Khuzaimah رَحِمَهُ اللهُ in his "Saheeh", by Ibne-Hibbaan رَحِمَهُ اللهُ in his "Saheeh" and by Haakeem رَحِمَهُ اللهُ in his "Mustadrak" that:
"Hadhrat Umm-e-Salimah رَضِىَ اللهُ عَنْهَا narrates, that Rasulullah صَلَّى اللهُ عَلَيْهِ وَسَلَّم taught a few words to her and that if these words are recited in Salaah, then whatever du'aa is made thereafter will be accepted. The words to recite are as follows: *Subhanallah* (10 times), *Alhamdulillah* (10 times) and *Allahu Akbar* (10 times)."

Reciting this three tasbeehaat 10 times each in the Salaatut Tasbih As-Sughra has no fixed place for its recitation. Hence, it is left to the choice of the Musalli (person performing this salaah) to recite this tasbeeh in whichever posture of salaah he wishes. He may also recite it after the completion of the last Tashah-hud.